IMAGINATION
ENGINEERING

IMAGINATION ENGINEERING

For organizations today, the rate of change is so high, you innovate or die. Not only this, but even after you've had one innovation win, you innovate and innovate again or you'll be dead in your competitors' waters. This book springs from our crazy times now when innovation must be a constant. If your journey into innovative territory is beginning, read it, for inspiration, for ideas and for practical help in starting the creativity habit.

HENRY BERRY, Director, Theory B Ltd

This is an excellent book, based on the premise that everyone is creative, but that creativity improves with practice ... A long overdue, practical manual for working 'smarter', not harder, by developing better solutions and ideas, through being more creative and having fun.

CAROLE LEE, Head of Innovations, Leo Burnett

In the era of the global market, when profound economic shifts are taking place and the intensity of competition is increasing in every trading sector, traditional management thinking becomes redundant. Many managers find themselves facing a business journey into the unknown, with few navigational aids for guidance. *Imagination Engineering* sets out to survey the new frontiers and find adventurous routes across otherwise hostile terrain. It is recommended reading for those in enterprise of every kind.

SIR COLIN MARSHALL, Chairman, British Airways

At last, creativity techniques that can be utilized within normal business processes. This is not just business as usual. Incrementalism is no longer acceptable. Creativity techniques such as these provide the means of generating significant benefits – not achievable by normal linear thinking.

MARK RALF, Director and Senior Vice President, Purchasing,
SmithKline Beecham

IMAGINATION ENGINEERING

A TOOLKIT FOR BUSINESS CREATIVITY

Paul Birch & Brian Clegg

FINANCIAL TIMES
Prentice Hall

London • New York • San Francisco • Toronto • Sydney • Tokyo • Singapore
Hong Kong • Cape Town • Madrid • Paris • Milan • Munich • Amsterdam

PEARSON EDUCATION LIMITED

Head Office:
Edinburgh Gate
Harlow CM20 2JE
Tel: +44 (0)1279 623623
Fax: +44 (0)1279 431059

London Office:
128 Long Acre
London WC2E 9AN
Tel: +44 (0)207 447 2000
Fax: +44 (0)207 240 5771
Website: www.business-minds.com

ISBN 0 273 64929 9

British Library Cataloguing in Publication Data
A CIP catalogue record for this book can be obtained from the British Library.

10 9 8 7 6 5 4 3 2 1

Typeset by Northern Phototypesetting Co. Ltd, Bolton
Printed and bound in Great Britain by Redwood Books, Trowbridge, Wiltshire

The Publishers' policy is to use paper manufactured from sustainable forests.

about the authors

BRIAN CLEGG

Born in Rochdale, Lancs, and educated at the Manchester Grammar School before getting MAs from Cambridge (Natural Sciences) and Lancaster (Operational Research). Spent 17 years with British Airways in a range of jobs including Business Support and Operational Research Manager and manager responsible for all personal computing. Promoted creativity initially within British Airways and later on a wider front. Has written two pieces of creativity software for BA. Author of over a dozen business books and regular columnist with *PC Week* and *Personal Computer World* magazines, Brian provides consultancy to corporates on business creativity, human/computer interface and flexible software development. Somehow he finds time to sing in several choirs and even see his family (a wife and two young daughters). He can be contacted at brian@cul.co.uk

PAUL BIRCH

Born in Chalfont St Giles, Bucks. Educated at Dr Challoners Grammar School, Amersham, degree at Newcastle Polytechnic, DMS at East Berks Management School and MBA at Lancaster University. Worked with British Airways for 17 years in a range of roles covering Operational Research, Information Technology, Marketing Finance, Strategy and most recently Corporate Jester. Developed an interest in creativity a few years ago when it became clear that the single largest differentiator which BA had in the marketplace was the creativity of its people. Has written articles, instructional pamphlets and books. Paul left BA a few years ago to set up a creativity consultancy. He can be contacted at Paul_S_Birch@msn.com

To Gillian and Frances for putting up with us while
we were writing this, and to Katy, Joanna, Chelsea,
and Rebecca for coping without us.

contents

IMAGINATION ENGINEERING – THE MAP

Surveying

The survey is where we establish our destination and surroundings, noting factors which may influence the decision or problem area. A known destination can be checked with the compass. If there is no clear goal, the level chain is ideal.

- **Compass** – Question stated directions. Ask "why?"
- **Obstacle map** – Identify blockages.
- **Level chain** – Find new destinations by moving up and down levels.
- **Aerial survey** – Collect information. Overview. Mind map.
- **Destination** – The problem is stated as "How to get to ...?".

Building

The building stage overcomes problems and obstacles on the way to a solution. Typically one or two techniques might be employed for a particular obstacle.

- **Tunnel** – Techniques which push through the obstacle. Challenging assumptions; distortion of facts; reversal of relationships.
- **Bridge** – Techniques that look at the problem from a different direction. Indulging in fantasy; taking the view of a different person or time; applying a metaphor.
- **By-pass** – Using a secondary destination to get around the blockage. Random word or picture, objects and nonsense.
- **New destination** – Sometimes it is more effective to go to another destination altogether. Second best solution.

Waymarking

When the route is established we need to mark the way, refining and clarifying. The waymarking stage may generate some extra building. Waymarking can be a private or public exercise to gather a range of views.

- **Slip road** – Slimming down possible solutions.
- **Washroom** – A purely subjective judgement: what do you feel about it?
- **Viewpoints** – Considering all stakeholders' views.
- **Signposts** – Looking at everything that's good.
- **Hazard markers** – Looking at what's wrong with the idea and suggesting ways to fix it.

Navigating

Having established the practicality of the idea and tuned it, it needs to be put into practice. Different navigation approaches are available for different types of problem.

- **The highway** – Where there is an obvious path and a detailed plan would be more obstacle than help. Requires a clear goal and few, broadly stated, milestones. There are slip roads to cope with changes due to outside influence.
- **The country lane** – Where there is no obvious path and more flexible planning is needed, the country lane provides the opportunity to think through each stage of the journey individually.
- **The railway** – Someone else is driving, but you will still keep track of progress. Agree route and stations to monitor progress against.
- **The river** – Very long-term goals, where the journey is daunting. This can only be achieved by rowing one stroke at a time, but holding in mind the destination.

key to margin symbols

 Interesting facts and figures.

 A book reference.

 An exercise.

 A reference to another relevant section in the book.

 Key thoughts or key words for the section.

 Biographical information.

 A quotation.

 Timeout – examples of creativity in action.

 Tale piece.

chapter one

WHAT'S IT ALL ABOUT?

■ **Introduction**

■ **Pioneering**

■ **Imagination engineering**

■ **Overkill?**
Surveying / Building / Waymarking / Navigating

INTRODUCTION

There are few things more frightening than the way many businesses react to creativity. It is treated with deep suspicion as the last resort of the marketing department; it is thought of as a strange quality exhibited by the long-haired types in an advertising agency, inappropriate for the rest of us. Yet creativity, properly managed, is a uniquely powerful tool for making things happen.

Most of our day-to-day decisions are based on experience, on re-using the pattern of the past. But experience can only take us so far. When a problem arises which has not been successfully solved before, it is often not enough to re-work an existing solution. Similarly, in the search for a new idea or a new product, we would be highly unlikely to come up with anything outstanding without a creative leap. And the pressures of the market can force frequent changes in a business in order to maintain a competitive edge. In all these circumstances, creativity can be a decisive weapon.

In recent years, a raft of techniques has been developed to enhance the creativity inherent in everyone, but these techniques are often used in a piecemeal fashion without any structure. Our aim is to pull together a simple, memorable, enjoyable approach for applying creativity, that runs from establishment of the problem through to implementation. We have called this approach Imagination Engineering.

If you want to apply creativity, you will be the sort of person who gets things done. For this reason, rather than loading the book up front with chapters of theory, we begin with a quick warm-up exercise in creativity, followed by a practical guide to using Imagination Engineering.

 **TIMEOUT**

Creativity in context

Though theory won't be allowed to dominate, we will be using frequent timeouts to examine some of the thinking that lies behind the creativity techniques you will be learning. Do you really care? It's up to you. You can ignore these sections, but to do so means missing out on an extra level of understanding. The choice is yours.

Some will contain examples of creativity in action. Unfortunately it's difficult to find fresh new examples which don't break professional confidences. For the most part, the really interesting new ideas which are being developed are not going to be included in a book like this. They are simply too useful to the firm that developed them to be made public.

Also, creative ideas very quickly become mainstream. Describing Sony's Walkman as a creative breakthrough loses some of its edge now that they are commonplace. Describing British Airways' Club World product as a service leap is not convincing now that most airlines in the world offer a similar product. On this theme, is there anyone in the world who still regards McDonald's as a neat new service process idea? It was once. What the examples should emphasise, however, is the potential for obtaining real benefit from creativity.

PIONEERING

Creativity is called for when seeking out a new goal or idea, or when faced with a new problem. There is a strong similarity between these challenges and those faced by the intrepid engineers who brought road and rail to virgin territory in the 19th century.

Searching for an idea involves a strong pioneer spirit. We are looking, in the words of a famous split infinitive, to boldly go where no-one has gone before. When problem solving, on the other hand, we are one step further down the line. We know where we are going, but there is an obstacle in our path. We need to find a way to get to the other side of the obstacle – or perhaps even to change our destination.

A word of warning here. An essential aspect of being a pioneer is not taking yourself too seriously. Real pioneers need a light, flexible touch to survive. While the creativity pioneer has less at stake, it's all too easy to try to counter the apparently wacky nature of some creativity techniques by being humorless. This won't help – in fact, we suggest it will actively hinder your creative growth.

IMAGINATION ENGINEERING

To help boost your creativity we have devised Imagination

"To boldly go" Part of the introduction to the TV program *Star Trek*. In the follow-up series, the phrase changed from "no man" to the politically correct "no-one."

Memory It is widely accepted that memory is not linear, but consists of multiply-linked chains of information, keyed to images.

Memory

For more information see Alan Baddeley, *Your Memory – A User's Guide* (Penguin, 1994).

Engineering, both as a framework to ease the creative process, and as a memory jogger. One of the hardest aspects of using creativity techniques is remembering them. By providing a strong, linked analogy, Imagination Engineering parallels the way memory works, making it easier to recall and employ the techniques.

We have split the process into four principal stages: **surveying**, **building**, **waymarking** and **navigating**. Get used to these terms; you are going to see a lot of them. The map on pages xii–xiii will help put them into context.

■ Surveying

Surveying

Covered in detail in Surveying, p. 23.

Surveying is the starting point of the process. Here we gather together the available information and assess the lie of the land. Part of our survey stage is to establish the end goal, if it is not already known. During surveying, techniques are available to structure the available data and to devise an appropriate goal.

■ Building

Building

Covered in detail in Building, p. 49.

Having established the destination, the next stage is building – constructing a route from A to B. Often there will be obstacles along the way, either forming the original problem or emerging from the surveying stage.

Here creativity techniques will be used to overcome the obstacle. This may involve tunneling through the blockage, bridging it, or going around it. It is even possible that we will need to totally change our goal and thus move away from the obstacle.

■ Waymarking

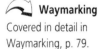

Waymarking

Covered in detail in Waymarking, p. 79.

The waymarking stage augments the outcome of building. Here we transform a basic route into a fully working transportation system. By looking at the advantages of the route, finding ways of overcoming the disadvantages, and balancing the facts with a subjective gut feel, we get over difficulties. As a result of the waymarking process it may be necessary to go back to one of the earlier stages; if not, a much more practical route will have been produced.

TIMEOUT

Why should we care?

The fact that you are reading this book indicates that you care about creativity. Have you ever thought about why it is important? Increasing your ability to generate creative ideas and creative solutions to problems will generate more money for your business. The two key sources of business advantage are cost reduction and product differentiation. These do not happen by chance: they are the result of creative thought. Many people will associate product differentiation and new product design with creative thinking. Few would see immediately how this applies to cost reduction. But costs do not reduce themselves. Differentiating the way you do business is just as important as differentiating the products you offer.

Whatever your task, generating creative ideas and creative solutions to problems can still remove obstacles from your path and make you more able to do the things you want. As Walt Disney said, "If you can dream it, you can do it." You may need some help along the way, you may need to work hard at it, you may even need to give up other things to pursue your dream. One thing is certain, you will need creative thinking to help you.

■ Navigating

This is navigating in the sense of progression – actually using the path that we have built. By this stage, we should have generated a good idea which is applicable to our problem or task. But in itself, an idea has no value – for business purposes. It has to be put into use to give a return. Often insufficient effort is put into implementation, so distinct navigation approaches are provided for different types of problem environment.

Navigating
Covered in detail in
Navigating, p. 91.

OVERKILL?

This highly structured approach is essential for a major business decision, but it may seem like overkill when something quick and dirty is required. It certainly would be if the whole process was followed slavishly, but Imagination Engineering is designed to be used flexibly. In a particular task, you may not need to go beyond idea generation:

Developed independently, our four stage process is similar to Roger von Oech's in *A Kick in the Seat of the Pants* (Harper and Row, 1986).

fine. It is quite possible to stop after the building stage, but at least you are taking a conscious decision to omit something. This would be true if, say, you wanted to generate the subject of a work of fiction or a pure idea. But in most business applications of creativity there is a need for more than this.

For a small, quick application, the stages need not be lengthy. We recommend that the survey is always employed, but it may amount to no more than spending a minute clarifying your task before plunging in – the old examiner's plea to read the question properly before proceeding. Once you get to know Imagination Engineering, you will be able to decide just how much to use in a particular problem, benefiting from the presence of the overall framework, but not hampered by a need to follow through a long, unnecessary process. There's nothing more frustrating than unnecessary procedures; you won't find them in Imagination Engineering.

Coming soon ➤➤➤

After the introductory exercises in the next chapter, we will look at the toolkit of Imagination Engineering. Each of the four stages has a set of techniques particularly appropriate to that part of the process. Beginning to sound dull? Don't worry, this is a business toolkit with a difference.

A Moral Tail

Each chapter of this book ends with a short work of fiction. This tale in a tail piece is multifunctional. It's there for fun – why not – and to aid your creativity. A short burst of fiction will help you to think in different ways. More than that, the content has been chosen to illustrate creativity in different ways. Some pieces were specially written for this book, others have been around for a while, as in this first example.

Some of the tales are science fiction – if this genre isn't usually of interest to you, please still give them a try. This style of writing is particularly useful in stimulating original thinking. It's up to you how you use the marginal notes here, as in the rest of the book, but we would recommend reading the main text first, then checking out the margin. That way you won't lose the flow.

Key words

Surveying; building; waymarking; navigating; framework.

Tails and tales

Lewis Carroll's mouse in *Alice's Adventures in Wonderland* provides a confusion between the mouse's tail and its story, emphasized by printing the tale in the shape of a tail.

FROM "THE HUNTING OF THE SNARK", FIT THE EIGHTH – THE VANISHING

By Lewis Carroll

They sought it with thimbles, they sought it with care;
  They pursued it with forks and hope;
They threatened its life with a railway-share;
  They charmed it with smiles and soap.

They shuddered to think that the chase might fail,
  And the Beaver, excited at last,
Went bounding along on the tip of its tail,
  For the daylight was nearly past.

"There is Thingumbob shouting!" the Bellman said,
  "He is shouting like mad, only hark!
He is waving his hands, he is wagging his head,
  "He has certainly found a Snark!"

They gazed in delight, while the Butcher exclaimed
  "He was always a desperate wag!"
They beheld him – their Baker – their hero unnamed –
  On the top of a neighbouring crag.

Erect and sublime, for one moment of time.
  In the next, that wild figure they saw
(As if stung by a spasm) plunge into a chasm,
  While they waited and listened in awe.

"It's a Snark!" was the sound that first came to their ears,
  And seemed almost too good to be true.
Then followed a torrent of laughter and cheers:
  Then the ominous words "It's a Boo–"

Then, silence. Some fancied they heard in the air
  A weary and wandering sigh
Then sounded like "–jum!" but the others declare
  It was only a breeze that went by.

For a full version of this nonsense masterpiece with splendid annotation by Martin Gardner, *The Annotated Snark* (Penguin, 1965) cannot be recommended too highly.

B names
The principal characters in the Snark all have names beginning with B, a device echoed in the 20th century fantasy Superman where three principal characters have the initials LL. Next time you are stuck for an idea, think of ten words beginning with the same letter and see what they inspire.

L names
In case Superman's L names are bugging you, they are Lois Lane, Lex Luthor and Lana Lang (his teenage sweetheart).

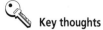 **Key thoughts**

- Keep a couple of books of nonsense rhyme as idea stimulators
- Beware the obvious first idea – the snark often is a boojum.

They hunted till darkness came on, but they found
  Not a button, or feather, or mark,
By which they could tell that they stood on the ground
  Where the Baker had met with the Snark.

In the midst of the word he was trying to say,
  In the midst of his laughter and glee,
He had softly and suddenly vanished away -
  For the Snark **was** a Boojum, you see.

GETTING STARTED

■ **Now go back ...**

■ **Practice makes easy**

■ **How was it for you?**

NOW GO BACK ...

If you skipped over the tale piece at the end of the previous chapter, let's dispose of your excuses before you go back and read it. You're too busy? How come you've got time to read this, then? Make time. This isn't the right time for frivolity? Wrong. You are never going to be creative unless any time can be the right time for frivolity. Anyway, there's a purpose to this. Can't read fiction in business hours? Why not, if it's to improve your business effectiveness. You've read it elsewhere? Read it again – this piece improves with re-reading and you need to look at it from a creativity standpoint. Whatever your excuse, go back now and read the tale piece. If you actually did read it without this prompting, congratulations, you've passed the first hurdle.

PRACTICE MAKES EASY

Creativity techniques become easier to use with practice. Before launching into the detail of Imagination Engineering, this section will help you to warm up your creative skills. In three exercises, each taking no more than five minutes, you will begin to use creativity more naturally.

These exercises use techniques extracted from the framework of Imagination Engineering. Don't worry about learning the techniques here – the rest of the book will deal with that – the aim is to become more comfortable with the feel of creativity. These exercises are much the same as an athlete's warm-up. They aren't the real thing, but they get the right muscles going.

Exercise 1 – The river

For the first exercise, imagine that you are standing on the bank of a river. It is fifteen feet wide. Your goal is to cross the river, without getting your feet wet. To help you cross it, you have been provided with a pencil. Take a minute out to give some thought as to how you can cross a fifteen foot wide river using only a single pencil.

If you haven't spent that minute's thought, do it now; don't go on

The feel of creativity
A good book for exercising your creative muscles is Edward de Bono *A Five Day Course in Thinking* (Penguin, 1968).

One minute
In one minute a humming bird's wings beat 4,200 times and a slug travels three inches. But at 1/36792000th of the average human lifespan, you can probably spare the time.

without it. One minute is not a lot of time and this will help you to move on.

It may be that you have come up with a way of crossing – if so, congratulations. If you are still waiting on the bank, don't worry. Let's look at a couple of solutions. What if the pencil was twenty feet long, reasonably wide, and made of a light, strong substance? You could span the river with it and walk across it. Or what if the pencil was a large, wooden, boat-shaped pencil? You could put it into the river, get in and paddle across with your hands.

If you are frustrated because this seems like cheating, relax. Creativity is about cheating – cheating your own assumptions and rules. It was never stated that the pencil was an ordinary pencil; you made that assumption. Don't dismiss these solutions because they are frivolous or impractical. That is the whole point. In using creativity techniques we often look for unnecessary assumptions, or temporarily suspend the rules, in order to get some insight into possible approaches which might still apply when the rules are restored.

Once you get over the irritation of being cheated, creativity can be great fun. Just as our enjoyment of humor depends on suspension of the rules of everyday life, so the employment of creativity, while aimed at a serious end, can be a very enjoyable process. Would you prefer it to be deadly boring?

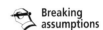 **Breaking assumptions**
How could you open a locked door with a pig?

 Humor
Check out mechanisms of humor in John Durant and Jonathan Miller (eds.), *Laughing Matters: A Serious Look at Humour* (Longman, 1988).

 The nature of creativity
See Arthur Koestler, *The Act of Creation* (Pan Books, London, 1966).

 **TIMEOUT**

What is creativity?

It is odd that creativity is a word which is so readily understood, yet is so hard to pin down. The chances are that anyone you speak to about creativity will have a different image to yours in mind. Perhaps it would be better to say that creativity is a word which is readily misunderstood. Interestingly, hard as it may be to define, it is easier to identify. Seeing an object, an event, or a piece of work, most people could give you an opinion as to whether or not it is creative.

One of the real difficulties with the word "creativity" is its broad spectrum. Few would disagree that Einstein's development of the theory of relativity was a creative act. Few would disagree that Michaelangelo's sculpture of David was a creative act. Are they linked? Do they need to be? The same word uncomfortably covers both acts. What we need is a

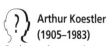

Arthur Koestler (1905–1983)
Budapest-born author who worked as a foreign correspondent around the world. He was imprisoned by Franco during the Spanish Civil War. In 1940 he came to England where he wrote a large number of books, including *The Act of Creation*. He killed himself in 1983.

description which can make sense of the ways in which the word is already used.

Arthur Koestler identified three creative types: The Sage, The Artist and The Jester who cover the three domains of creativity, Discovery, Art and Humor. To make them more memorable we have called these areas the Ah Ha!, Aahh!, and Ha Ha! of creativity. Inspiration, or discovery, is what we most often see as creativity. Most readers of this book will be reading in order to improve their ability to generate creative ideas or improve their ability to find creative solutions to problems. Few will have seen it as a path to improving their artistic talent or their ability to create jokes. Indeed, our concentration will be upon business problem solving and innovation stimulation but we would argue that developing a creative approach to life will develop all of these areas. In further timeouts we will look at these three domains in more depth.

Exercise 2 – Shoplifting

The first exercise was something of a shock tactic, used more to get the heart rate up than to be particularly productive. In this second exercise, we will be using another creativity technique, but applying it to a more practical business problem. Shoplifting is endemic in the retail world. While expensive tagging systems and monitors can reduce shoplifting, it still manages to chip a sizable chunk from the profits.

Random word technique
For more information, see Building, p. 66.

In this exercise we are going to look at ways to reduce losses through shoplifting. In Imagination Engineering terms, shoplifting is an obstacle to achieving expected profits, so we need a way to get around it. One of the techniques in Imagination Engineering involves the use of a random word to stimulate ideas. If you were doing this exercise for real, you would first generate that random word. As this is a warm-up exercise, we have chosen one. It should be emphasized that this word was not picked to fit the problem; to do so would have limited creativity by imposing preconceptions.

The word is NURSERY. It is worth spending a few minutes jotting down some associations with this word – what a nursery is like, what it makes you think of.

Now come back to the problem. What is there about a nursery and your associations which might be applied to reducing shoplifting? Don't worry about practicalities; we are still at the cheating stage. Use your nursery ideas as wildly and dramatically as you like. You should get together at least half a dozen different ideas.

Now look through your ideas. This is where rationality returns. Is there anything practical which is suggested by those ideas? Could some off-the-wall concept be modified to become realistic? Or is there some new approach that leaps out at you, hinted at by one of these ideas? If you haven't actually done the exercise yet, go back and do it before reading the next paragraph.

We spent a few minutes playing with this idea and came up with two major associations with the word nursery – a place in which to look after children, and a place to grow and sell plants. From these the following associations developed: restrain, supervise, play with, give toys, educate, keep breakables out of reach, nurture, fertilize, propagate, sell plants, make profit, pots, confine, telephone orders (and many more – we had a few sheets of paper with rambling associations).

"Restrain" and "supervise" made us think of putting more staff and more detectives in the store, or installing more cameras (or just camera boxes). A wilder thought was that we might tie our customers' hands together to prevent them shoplifting. That is not practical, but does give rise to looking at ways of keeping their hands busy during shopping, or minimising the ability to take an item.

"Giving toys" inspired putting worthless but apparently valuable items in the spots where shoplifting is liable to occur. It also made us think of charity bins where toys are donated. Some shoplifters steal simply for the thrill of getting away with it. Why not provide a shoplifter's wall safe, where they can drop things they've stolen but don't actually want? It is often this sort of idea on the fringe of sanity which eventually is refined into a winning solution.

"Educate" made us think of a poster campaign aimed at casual or first-time shoplifters, emphasizing the penalties. "Telephone orders" and "deliveries" made us think of changing our distribution strategy so that our stock is warehoused and the customers buy from catalogues or home computers. The overall concept of looking after children made us think that where young people are responsible for

---

Nursery
1. Room or place for children and their nurses.
2. Practice, institution, sphere, place in or by which qualities or classes of people are fostered or bred.
3. Plot of ground in which young plants are reared for transportation, esp. trees etc. for sale; fish rearing pond; place where animal life is developed.
4. Grouped balls (*Concise Oxford Dictionary*, OUP).

Creative solutions
Need not be wacky or odd. Creativity often involves a temporary suspension of normality, but the adopted solution can be entirely ordinary. Indeed, with hindsight, a creative solution will almost always seem ordinary.

shoplifting, a free entertainment arcade might tempt them away from our goods.

In this exercise we employed a creativity technique to break out of our normal mode of thinking; it isn't natural to involve a nursery in ways of reducing shoplifting. We then pulled back to a practical route towards our goal. Don't worry if you didn't come up with an earth-shattering new approach; the point is to get in the practice.

Exercise 3 – What goes up ...

This third exercise looks at the fortunes of an umbrella company. This hypothetical company has a good, solid market in umbrellas, but is being undercut by foreign imports. Our company cannot produce at costs which will enable us to match the prices of our competitors. Instead, we must find new product lines or a new marketing approach which will boost sales.

In this exercise, while we know what our goal is about – some way of increasing sales – we don't know what the goal actually is, so we will be employing a surveying technique called the level chain to look for new opportunities. In using the level chain we build a progression of possibilities, starting from our existing state. Each link in the chain can move up a level, to something more abstract – so from an umbrella we could move up to rainwear – or we can move down a level, to something more specific – from an umbrella this might be a folding umbrella or a plastic umbrella.

Random changes in level are added to the chain until we hit on something which generates an idea. Usually this will take no more than four or five links. Here's one we made earlier:

 Level chain
For more information, see Surveying, p. 32.

 "Here's one we made earlier"
Catch phrase of BBC children's program *Blue Peter* which has become part of the (UK) English language.

> An umbrella – (up a level to)
>
> A roof – (down a level to)
>
> A tile – (down a level to)
>
> A Mah Jong tile

 Loose links
Note that there is no need to be too precise in your linkages. An umbrella is a roof, sort of. A tile is a specific part of a roof, rather than a specific type of roof.

Mah Jong, of course, is a game. Now there isn't much of a youth market in umbrellas at the moment. Why not start producing umbrellas with built-in games, which would make them much more attractive to young people? Notice how the level changes were quite random, as was the decision to stop at a game, simply because an idea struck us.

Now try two or three chains for yourself (it's best to do this on a piece of paper). Start with an umbrella and try going up and down levels until something strikes you as usable. If your chains get too long, start again.

Hopefully you will now have some level chains of your own. Here's another example we worked through:

> An umbrella – (up a level to)
>
> A roof – (down a level to)
>
> A shop roof – (down a level to)
>
> A tie shop roof

Tie shops work because ties are a fashion accessory, with the result that you don't just need one tie, but many, different, jazzy ties. Why not take the same approach with umbrellas – make it the done thing to have a range of umbrellas for different occasions and moods. You could change the designs seasonally, and market an expensive handle with interchangeable, detachable tops. In this case we used the same first link as before, but came up with a totally different idea. Both these chains started by moving up a level, but they could as easily have started downwards.

This second chain, which was generated without any forethought, is a remarkably strong echo of the strategy undertaken by a Swiss company in coming up with Swatch. Substitute watches for umbrellas in the scenario above and a real life case emerges. Swatch may not have been devised using a creativity technique, but it is interesting that the concept could be generated so easily with the appropriate methods.

 The tie shop
Why a tie shop? The image of a shop (roof) generated a picture of our local shopping street, at the top of which is a tie shop. Use pictures in your mind to help create links.

 Swatch
The Swiss watch industry was in decline, collapsing under the pressure of cheap Far Eastern competition until Swatch was conceived, totally transforming the sales image of a watch.

 **TIMEOUT**

Ah Ha!

It is instructive to look at how creative ideas are generated. Some do seem to arrive as a bolt from the blue whereas others are quite obviously the result of a considerable amount of painstaking work. Even the bolts from the blue do not really arrive fully formed in your head with no effort.

Have you ever noticed how you can push really hard for a breakthrough in a particular area and have no success until sometime after you've given up, when the inspiration hits? The fact is you never stopped working on the issue. You may have consciously moved on to other things but the final idea came about as a result of the work that your subconscious was doing in the background. It is often a useful technique to research a particular area and then leave it for a week before going further. This will allow your subconscious the opportunity to structure your thoughts and to work on interesting, unusual approaches.

If your objective is to generate creative ideas, there are a number of approaches open to you. The first is to sit and think. In general, if you have not mastered the art of idea generation you will find that your success is limited. The second approach is to cram into your head all of the data that you might need to address the problem and then leave it alone. You are likely to have further thoughts as a result of the work your subconscious does. This approach is pretty hit and miss for most of us. The third approach is the most structured. That is to work with a technique or range of techniques aimed at improving your ability to generate ideas. This is often the most effective approach. The techniques covered in this book will give you a useful tool bag; they are by no means the only ones available.

As you work more and more at generating ideas and creative solutions to problems, you will find that you become more effective even without resorting to formal techniques. This is because the techniques which you use are all aimed at removing the obstacles which you or others place in the path of your own creativity. Practice with these techniques makes you more able to remove obstacles in the future without obviously using techniques. Eventually, like the master carpenter who no longer has to think of their interaction with the wood they shape, you will not need to think of removing obstacles; the techniques and processes will become internalised and a part of the way you think. Creativity is like any other skill, the more you use it, the better you get.

HOW WAS IT FOR YOU?

That quick foray into creativity should have given a feeling for the power of what seem to be simple tricks. Creativity techniques transform a problem by providing a different viewpoint. It is very easy to get tunnel vision and be hemmed in by practice and experience. Some while ago, while running a creativity session with a group of eleven-year-olds in a school, we tried introducing them to creativity techniques. The class found it very difficult to grasp the concept of a technique, until one of them put forward the picture of a pickaxe. The technique acts as a pickaxe, to break out of our boxed-in, habitual path and open up a new one.

Putting creativity into practice requires a suitable technique as a pickaxe, but we also need a structure to help move from an initial breakthrough to implementation. The next sections will fit the techniques we've used, and others, into the overall framework of Imagination Engineering. To make it easier to keep track of these techniques and the framework, and to provide a quick reminder, we have summarized the contents of the four Imagination Engineering stages in the map on pages xii–xiii.

Coming soon ➤➤➤

The starting point for the civil engineer is a survey. In the next chapter we launch into the first section of the Imagination Engineering framework – a survey which will build up a picture of where we are and where we want to go. In some cases it may even generate a solution, but mostly it is laying foundations for the future.

Creativity in schools

Creativity is not widely taught as a classroom subject in the UK and USA but Edward de Bono has worked widely in Australian schools.

Key words

Pickaxe; cheating assumptions; techniques.

 **TALE PIECE**

OBSERVATIONS

By Brian Clegg

 A different view

Taking a look at a problem from a different viewpoint is often valuable. Be prepared to be extreme in your choice of viewpoint. Why not a plant's view?

It's not easy being a nasturtium. There's no conversation from you lot. I mean, someone might say "what a pretty nasturtium" as they look round the garden, but that hardly constitutes intellectual stimulus. Anyway, it smacks of being the horticultural equivalent of a sex object, a centerfold flower – they certainly aren't interested in me for my mind.

If you're wondering how I know what they say, there's nothing wrong with my hearing. It's obvious I can't see – I haven't got eyes, have I? – but I hear perfectly well. Vibrations in the stamens, quite a sensitive pickup with a big bell horn like … oh, compost, here comes a bee. I don't mind it in principle, it's all good natural stuff, but when it gets inside it tickles something wicked. And I can't help feeling violated, you know? Ooh, careful there. These bumble bees are so clumsy; give me a honey bee any day.

Where was I? Oh, yes, the senses. You don't have to feel sorry for me because I can't see. I smell too – not like a rose, snailbrain, I mean I have a sense of smell – I have a sense of touch and I'm sensitive to a whole range of the electromagnetic spectrum. It doesn't give me that prissy, focussed clarity that the eye seems to have, but I can interpret the shapes pretty well and I see your heat and the radio noise from your motors; all sorts of things beyond your vision.

I can understand it coming as a bit of a shock, finding out that a plant is sentient, but don't go jumping to conclusions. The whole garden isn't teeming with intellect. You don't hear great debates coming from the herbaceous border or poetry emerging from a holly bush. It's only us nasturtiums that are different and that's because we aren't really plants; not as you expect them to be. We didn't evolve like this. Well, I suppose we did evolve, unless our fundamentalists are right and we were created by a supreme shrub from a drop of his ineffable nectar, but what I'm trying to say is that we didn't evolve in the sunny gardens of suburbia from a perfectly ordinary rootstock.

Ineffable

Unutterable, too great for description in words; that must not be uttered
(*Concise Oxford Dictionary*, OUP).

What the hell does ineffable mean, is what I say. It's the sort of guff I hear all the time. I only got planted next to a Jehovah's Witness, didn't I. You can't imagine what it's like, being asked every morning if you've thought about God lately. I can't get away; I've twisted my stem as much as I can in an attempt to get behind that cracked flowerpot on the patio, but the bastard follows me. He's not really a Jehovah's Witness – I mean he's a nasturtium after all – but he would be if he were human. The only advantage I've got over you when you get caught at the front door in your pyjamas at ten o'clock on a Saturday morning is that he can't sell me a copy of *The Watchtower*. No hands.

And I still don't know what ineffable means. It sounds like swearing somehow, but it feels more like a smell. I asked him once outright, old God Squad, and he came up with a perfect circular argument. God's nectar is ineffable. What does ineffable mean? It means having the nature of God's nectar, of course. Very enlightening. He moved quickly onto the bit of scripture that shows (according to him) that only the few will be saved and packeted up in a seed bag for the second coming.

How did I get onto this? Evolution, wasn't it? Prepare yourself for a shock; we are not of this world. I know you say the same about Jehovah's Witnesses, but that's not the point; I mean we're extra-terrestrial. Not like ET – I don't go around wanting to phone home or anything; this is home. I suppose you're wondering how I know about ET. I can't claim to be an expert on Spielberg, but I keep up on the contemporary cinema. It's the girl, you see, the one from the house. When the weather's good she brings one of those little portable TV things out onto the lawn and when it's not so good she has the window wide open. She always watches Barry Norman.

Barry Norman
Film critic and former host of Britain's longest running film review TV show.

There I go, surprising you again, dropping household names. Just because I'm a nasturtium doesn't mean I know nothing about world affairs. Why, only the other day the front cover of *Hello* magazine blew across my bed. I not only know of Barry Norman – he reviews films and models sweaters – but I can tell the difference between Madonna and Margaret Thatcher. I can't remember which one's supposed to be the goody and which the baddy, but I can tell them apart, which is more than many nasturtiums can.

To be frank, and it's embarrassing because I'm talking about my own kind, nasturtiums are people-ist. They say things like "they all look the same to me" and "they're only animals, after all" and they call you blubberies and clodhoppers and other terms of abuse. It isn't fair, because once you get to know people they're quite different from one another; maybe not as individual as nasturtiums, but they have marked traits. I'm sure you have too. And I know it's not true that you all live by eating animal flesh, that's a foul distortion put around by extremists. As for all being the same, I can often tell what sex someone is without even using my sense of smell.

Sex – now that's something I'll never understand. Like I said, I can relate intellectually to bees, but who could enjoy it? Enjoyment is another thing entirely. And yet humans allow their whole lives to be dominated by an obsession with sex. I suppose that's why they don't have such a rich and contemplative culture as our own. They're too busy bonking to give much thought to art. Certainly that's the case if the TV's anything to go by. Mind you, it never seems to happen in our back yard, unless you count that little incident behind the shed; I never really got to the bottom of that.

We, of course, live our art. We are our art, in fact. I don't mean the colored petals – a pretty face is a pretty face, art doesn't come into it – but the shapes we describe as we grow can be the highest form of expression. That's if you aren't more concerned about avoiding your fundamentalist neighbor than adding a third counter spiral to your main stem. That prat is personally responsible for my lack of cultural development; I should sue him.

Hello, here comes the cat again. I suppose they seem fun to you, just furry little bundles, but from down here the world is very different. You never know when you're going to be sprayed with some foul smelling fluid or half dug up to make room for some sordid waste products. That's one thing you animals have never got right. We mostly pump out oxygen; it's invisible, odor free and generally regarded as useful. What did you ever find to do with cat shit?

Ah. No problem, it was just following the scent of a bird that passed through earlier, no doubt after the proverbial worm. We nasturtiums have proverbs too, but I have to say it is one area where humanity seems to have the edge. "Too many cooks spoil the broth" and "people who live in glass houses shouldn't throw stones" don't have much competition from "too many leaves makes for poor petals except when the soil is particularly rich or weather conditions unusually favourable". Nasturtium literature is not renowned for its pithiness.

I haven't really explained about us being extra-terrestrial, have I? You might have wondered why it's so easy to grow nasturtiums; how you've only got to show us a bit of soil and we bounce up all over the place. The thing is, when your seeds are used to entering the earth's atmosphere and plummeting in free fall without so much as a thistledown parachute and slamming into any old bit of soil, you've got to be adaptable.

Not that we all are. Some nasturtiums have become very fussy. It's the political activists, you see. You probably put it down to the wrong sort of soil or not enough water and sun: something suitably environmental. Anthers to that. They're stroppy buggers, that's what it is. They come out of their seeds demanding certain rights and they're not going to grow unless they get them. And since no-one but us other, poor, uncomplaining nasturtiums gets to hear them, nothing gets done and they die sorry deaths.

Death's a difficult one, of course. Life and death; water and drought. I mean, forgetting old second coming next door, it's a bit of a puzzler. We don't hang around for long in human terms, I can see that. At least I assume you're telling the truth, but maybe it's like sex – everyone lies about it so much that no-one's sure what the truth really is. What I do know is we come into this world well endowed with genetic memory, and by the time we're flowering we're adults (my neighbor apart). Then along comes autumn, whatever that is, and zap, you've had it. It makes you think. Couldn't someone do away with autumn?

I'm churning all this into my root structure and I don't suppose any of you humans are going to have the intelligence to decode it, but you've got to leave something for posterity. Even if you could decode it, I suppose it'd be

Great rejections of our time
This story was rejected by a US science fiction magazine with the wonderful (if unimaginative) line "We will never publish a story written from the viewpoint of a nasturtium."

considered a hoax. I mean, you aren't entirely receptive to the concept of intelligent plants from another planet. Having said that, there was the John Wyndham business, but really! I certainly wouldn't want to share a bed with a triffid, would you? It's downright exploitation of plants. It's not us who go around mangling and eating other creatures. Okay, so there's a few carnivores among us, but they're the black sheep of the family. You never see a carnivorous plant at a garden party or a wedding, do you?

What I'm trying to say is, don't go bracketing us with triffids in your mind. Let's face it, they were pretty unlikely, weren't they? Isn't there too much suspension of disbelief required to cope with a dirty great stinging plant that can walk? Humans can take a lot away from us, but not the dignity of immobility. I should imagine a triffid would look positively ludicrous. But wait, what vibrations through yonder garden path echo? It is the east and some human or other is the sun. I draw the line at calling you clodhoppers, but I have to agree you're heavy footed. It's like a small earthquake.

You'll have noticed the subtle literary reference there, unless you read the newspaper that is convinced that Elvis is still singing somewhere on the dark side of the moon. It may come as some surprise to you to know that I have a wide and incisive knowledge of Complete William Shakespeare Revision. Of course, Revision was one of your greatest writers, so maybe even the scandal sheet readers would have heard of him. He may well have worked on the Mary Tyler Moore Show back in the early days.

Whatever, Revision must have been a great man to become famous with a name like that. My expert knowledge originates from the girl in the house, who was reading up for examinations back in my youth. She used to sprawl on the grass with her course book and read vast chunks of Revision's greatest hits out loud. I can't help but suspect he was a nasturtium himself. Not only was he unusually intelligent for a human, he had the nasturtium way of never using five words when ten will do.

But this is distracting from my reportage of the present. It's not the girl this time, it's the other female, the one with the more extensive clothing. Probably got something to hide – we nasturtiums say "if you've got it, flaunt it," or more precisely "if you have the sort of petals that make you stand out in the crowd or if you have a beautifully formed stem, get out from under that cloche and stun the lot of them," which as usual lacks conciseness. She's coming right up to us; bending over the bed.

I know you make a lot of fuss about faces, but really they are the most unattractive blurs. I think the human race would be a lot better off if it concentrated more on ankles. From here, I'd say that they were your best feature. But anyway, she's thrusting this blobby face thing at me. The eyes are most odd, they change the light in a distressing way. She's feeling me up! The cheek of it; what sort of pervert is she? She's running her fingers over

John Wyndham Parkes Lucas Beynon Harris (1903–1969)
Popular and prolific science fiction author, probably best known for his disaster novels like *The Day of the Triffids*, which dwelt on the reaction of middle class England to unexpected upheaval. The triffids were mobile, carnivorous plants.

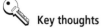

Key thoughts

- Be original in taking a look through other eyes
- Never say "never"
- Simile is powerful.

my petals. Give me a bee anytime, this is downright unpleasant. Now she's … ouch.

I really don't know what to say. She's only pulled my head off. I'm not going to be able to add much more; I don't need to be physically connected to the stem to code my roots, but I can't live long like this. What's the big idea? I see them cutting flowers, the flashy numbers like the roses, but at least they have the grace to leave them a bit of stem. She just twisted my head straight off. The only consolation, if it's possible to be consoled when you've had your head pulled off, is she got the Jehovah's Witness too. Let's see him be holier than thou now, eh.

Mostly I can only see sky, though she's joggling us around. Lots of sky … then a wall – so that's what's behind the shed. What's this? We're going into the house. I know all about houses, but I've never seen one; perhaps she's feeling remorse and she's going to show me round before I pop off. She's turning me over a bit; I can see ahead. Oh no. This is too much. I demand a refund. How would you like to end up as a garnish on a bloody salad? I could curl up and …

chapter
three

SURVEYING

Mapping

An interesting discussion of mental mapping can be found in Michael B. McCaskey, *Mapping, The Executive Challenge* (Pitman 1982) reprinted in Jane Henry, *Creative Management* (Sage, 1991).

 Framework

See the introduction on p. 4 for a view of where Surveying fits. You can also check the map of the Imagination Engineering framework in Chapter 6.

 Framework

For a fuller discussion of problems see Arthur Vangundy, *Techniques of Structured Problem Solving* (Van Nostrand Reinhold Co. Inc., 1988).

 Bishop Berkeley (1685–1753)

Clergyman and philosopher George Berkeley suggested that matter (e.g. trees in a forest) did not exist without a mind to be aware of it.

THE LIE OF THE LAND

The world is a mess. This is not a political or philosophical statement, it is a fact. Most people like order and structure, and so spend a great deal of their time rearranging their world view to fit accepted patterns. We are great at making sense of things, but not nearly so good at using our understanding to find creative solutions to our problems. Surveying, the first stage of Imagination Engineering, will help you to make sense of the world without closing down your options for the future.

We all map the world in our heads, continually making sense of the unknown by fitting it into a mental model of reality. As we learn more, the detail that we can fill in becomes sharper. It is rather like the early European maps of the New World. Initially, very small areas of coastline were covered. Progressively the coastline became more accurate and detailed. Eventually the interior started to be known and, consequently, mapped. This surveying process took hundreds of years. You will need to accomplish your surveys in far less time, cutting centuries of surveying down to a few hours, or in some cases, minutes.

The overview of Imagination Engineering will have given you a picture of where surveying fits into the framework. Before you start to produce creative ideas, you must understand where your problem fits into the world, and generate a statement that encapsulates your problem or need for a creative idea.

Throughout this book we will be talking about creative problem solving and idea generation. To avoid repetition of this clumsy phrase we will refer simply to problem solving – making the need for a new idea simply another problem.

A problem is a gap between the way things are and the way you would like them to be. This gap could be something which you see as a problem (creative problem solving) or as an opportunity for improvement (creative idea generation). Rather like Bishop Berkeley's trees, the gap does not exist to be removed unless you see it; the problem cannot be solved unless you recognise it as such. You and your understanding are key elements in this activity.

It might appear obvious that you must know what a problem is before you can solve it. Experience does not support this observation. Many attempts at solving a problem have failed before they have even started, as a result of defining the problem in a way that precludes the best solutions. A clear statement of the problem can often be one of the most powerful tools available in moving forward.

Don't skip over this phase of problem solving. It is surprising how easy it is to satisfy yourself that you have thought deeply enough about the construction of your problem, only to find at a later stage that your original assumptions were questionable. Even experienced problem solvers tend to be very good at idea generation and at encouraging others to rush into generating ideas. They may overlook the stage which lays the foundations for this.

Peter was walking past his friend John's house when he saw John on his hands and knees, under a street lamp outside his front gate.

"What are you doing, John?" he asked.

"I'm looking for my house keys," replied John, obviously extremely drunk. Peter, a helpful sort of person, squatted down and started to help. After fifteen minutes of fruitless searching, Peter asked: "OK, where exactly did you drop these keys?"

"On my doorstep," said John.

"So why are we looking out here?" asked Peter in exasperation.

"Because this is where the light is, of course."

You don't have to be drunk to find yourself looking in the wrong place or searching for the wrong goal. It happens all the time. Sometimes it is because you have been misled by others, as Peter was by John. More often it is because you have misled yourself. Taking time out for a quick survey will repay itself many times over.

Surveying is about developing a clear statement of your problem which does not close off possible creative solutions. This stage of the Imagination Engineering process involves both divergent thought and convergent thought. Overall, the survey you conduct will give you a clear picture of the lie of the land, and allow you to decide how to move forward.

10 minutes
If you have little time, you will still find that you produce better results, quicker, by using these techniques. You do not need to use them all – the more you use, the wider will be your options later. Look for the 10 minute notes for clues to short cuts.

Divergent and convergent thought
Thought processes which expand possibilities and broaden the scope are known as divergent. Thought processes which focus in on particulars and narrow the scope are known as convergent. Creativity involves both styles of thinking.

TIMEOUT

Artistic creativity

An excellent book is Betty Edwards' *Drawing on the Right Side of your Brain* (Collins, 1986). She covers specific techniques which will help you to draw and help you to see what you are drawing as it really is. Many of her techniques are applicable to any form of art.

Toolkit

Each of the main areas of Imagination Engineering contains a toolkit of techniques to support the activity.

Aahh!

There are business applications for art. The advertising business could not exist without it. Company publications rely on it. In general, however, it is considered divorced from business life. Perhaps it should not be so swiftly dismissed. Aside from the obvious aesthetic value of a rounded existence which includes an appreciation of beauty, we all make use of art in our everyday business. A well-presented page of text can be regarded as a creative output. In Koestler's terms, it is artistic creativity. Similarly the graphics we use to support a presentation are a form of art. Many of the things we do on a day-to-day basis are artistically creative acts. The creativity may be of a low order in comparison to the Sistine Chapel but is, nevertheless, important to success and essential to business.

Much of the process of creating something aesthetic is quite different to problem solving or idea generation. In the early stages there may be some overlap of approach to generate the ideas behind the art. Overall, however, problem solving is different. This book will not help much with artistic creativity, but it is covered in great depth elsewhere.

SURVEYING TOOLKIT

■ Summary

The tools we will use to gather facts and narrow our focus to a specific problem are:

- **The compass** – checking position and direction by repeatedly asking "Why?"
- **The obstacle map** – identifying blockages that sit between our current position and our goal.
- **The level chain** – shifting away from our current position by moving up and down levels until we discover a new direction.
- **The aerial survey** – drawing a map of the problem area to gain an understanding of relationships and the background to your current area of focus.
- **The destination** – confirming our direction by phrasing it as a "How to ..." statement.

You will probably not make use of all of these tools when surveying for yourself. There is no reason not to, but time constraints may force you to limit your activity. Whichever you do decide to use, make sure that you include the destination. Without a clear statement of the problem, your later activities will be unfocussed.

■ The compass

The compass is a tool for checking your direction. It allows you to compare the way you are actually going with your intention. In the real world, you use a compass to check direction against a single fixed point on the Earth's surface. In our analogy it is a way of questioning your understanding while defining a problem. The difficulty with this technique is that it is so simple and so obvious that you will tend not to bother with it. This is a mistake.

The technique

The technique simply involves asking, "Why?" That's all there is to it! This is so simple that it may seem unsurprising that the technique is not much used, but don't underestimate the value of this approach. Remember that when you were three years old you gained much of your understanding of the world by asking your parents "Why?" over and over and over again. Our approach is much the same. Make the question recursive, continuing to ask it until you've reached a nonsense level. Once you have tried this as a way of broadening your understanding of a problem you will be surprised at the power hidden behind this simple facade.

To be more specific, having stated your problem, or your objective, question it by asking why. Say you had decided to increase output by 10 percent; using the compass you would ask why you wanted to do so. Repeat the question on your answers until you get some insight or you are bogged down. Even if this has given you a useful approach, go back and start again. Start with the same problem statement, or recast it, and go through the whole process once more.

In order to strengthen the power of the linked analogy that surrounds Imagination Engineering it is important to associate the compass technique with asking the question, "Why?" Make sure that you have this link firmly established before going forward.

Compass
The magnetic compass has been used in a simple form for at least 700 years.

10 minutes
Asking "Why?" takes very little time. If you are really pushed you can hold the conversation in your head and only write down the conclusions you draw.

Five Ws and H

For more on Ws and H (Whys and How) see Arthur Vangundy's, *Techniques of Structured Problem Solving* (Van Nostrand Reinhold Co. Inc., 1988).

The two of us thought that we were pretty smart in developing the notion of asking the question why as a technique. Since then we have discovered Arthur Van Gundy's "Why Method." This uses exactly the same approach of continually checking and re-evaluating direction through questions. We still may be pretty smart, but sadly this won't prove it!

Example

Our first example involves questioning a direction, though the compass can probe any aspect of the mess that surrounds your problem.

You are a teacher responsible for a class of eleven-year-old children. You want to develop an interesting approach for teaching some mathematical concepts. Below is the monologue which might take place when using the compass to check direction. If you want to try the technique for yourself before reading the worked example, take some time out now and play around with this notion.

The right answer

One of the hardest tasks in becoming more creative is moving away from the search for a single right answer. There is very rarely a single answer.

I want to find a more interesting way of teaching mathematics to eleven-year-old children.
  Why?
Because it is my job.
  Why?
Because I love to teach.
  Why?
Because imparting knowledge really motivates me.
  Why?
Because when I am doing this I feel that I am being really useful.
  Why?
Because basic mathematics is essential to living in modern society and I believe that teaching this well gives my class a better chance.

That's probably far enough for this chain. We have stopped at this point, not because we have reached a conclusion, but because we got bored. We should now restart the process and, as long as we give ourselves a different first answer, we would take a totally different route. In the example above we played it straight and answered the questions sensibly. Don't do this all of the time. The question is pretty stupid, perhaps the answer should be too. If a silly answer pops into your head then put that down. There are no right or wrong answers to this.

Once you have developed a few lists of questions and answers, look them over for further directions. Just the single short list above suggests a couple of ideas. The final remark that mathematics is essential in everyday life suggests linking the concepts being taught to everyday situations. This is not particularly novel but it might not have been the approach you would have taken without prompting.

If imparting knowledge motivates you, what are you doing to make sure that your work involves this? It is all too easy to concentrate on delivering the curriculum without achieving any personal satisfaction. Remember, these are not solutions, they are merely possible directions. The solutions come later.

Example

Let's take a look at a more business based example. In this instance we use the compass to check our understanding of the world.

You run a small hotel in a tourist resort. Your hotel used to be fully booked for more than a year ahead. It is now taking you more time and more effort to fill the rooms. The hotel is still full, so this is not a problem in itself, but you are concerned that the world is changing enough to present a problem in the future. There is also the ever present thought that you might be able to make more money if you were able to run your business differently. So, let's begin.

 Compass
What was the first thing you did after getting up this morning? Apply the compass to it.

My hotel is not fully booked before the year is finished.
   Why?
Perhaps because people are booking later.
   Why?
Perhaps they are waiting for later booking bargains.
   Why?
They do not have as much money to spend on their holidays.
   Why?
They may be having more than one holiday.
   Why?

> Leisure is becoming more important and people are fussier about what they do with their leisure time.
> *Why?*
> People expect more choice.

Holidays

Travel and tourism generates almost three and a half trillion US dollars (1995) with a third of this in the European Union.

We'll stop at this point and log the thought that we might not be offering the choices that people want in their holidays. Perhaps one direction for creative thinking should be to broaden the choices of holiday we offer. We should also log that we do not understand the motivation of the hotel's customers as well as a good business person should. Perhaps we should give some thought to ways of collecting more facts from our customers.

In order to emphasise the point about doing this more than once as a way of gaining understanding, let us run through this example one more time.

Devon reality

We have since come across a hotel in Devon offering exactly this service. Cottages – ideal for families – in the grounds of a luxury hotel with access to its facilities. This approach is already quite popular in the US.

> My hotel is not fully booked before the year is finished.
> *Why?*
> Maybe not as many people want to stay in hotels.
> *Why?*
> Perhaps they are using alternative accommodation.
> *Why?*
> Perhaps they prefer self-catering holidays.
> *Why?*
> It may give them more freedom from the restrictions of the hotel.

Knowing when to stop

With practice you will become comfortable with choosing a stopping place. To start with, try using five "Whys" and stopping to look back over your results.

Again, let's stop here. The view of our mythical hotelier before starting this process was that people would prefer a hotel holiday to a self-catering holiday because the hotel does much of the work that they would otherwise have to do for themselves. By going through this process we have arrived at a position where it is possible to imagine people preferring self-catering holidays because of the freedom they offer. Perhaps an area of creative thought should be how we can offer the freedom of a self-catering holiday in a hotel.

This might mean freedom from fixed meal times, or from the embarrassment of a maid entering the room – we don't know yet. Remember, the compass is getting you to a position where you have a better understanding of directions. It is not choosing a direction and it is not solving your problems. It helps clarify your position in the world.

Dyed fabric

At DuPont they had to develop a fire resistant Nomex aramid fiber, that could be dyed without requiring special procedures in customers' mills. The material's tight structure baffled researchers until one asked what made it possible to enter a coal mine. The answer was props that keep the tunnel from collapsing. Applying the mining metaphor, they were able to change the molecular structure of the Nomex to allow dyes to enter while the fibers were "propped up." As a result, an easily colored, flame resistant fabric is available for use in aircraft interiors.

TIMEOUT

◼ The obstacle map

Not all applications of creativity involve overcoming obstacles, though practically any decision, idea generating session or problem solving exercise can be phrased in terms of an obstacle to you achieving your desired state.

The obstacle map offers no real suggestions for overcoming your obstacles, but helps the process by making these obstacles explicit.

Every problem an opportunity

The idea that every creativity application has an obstacle is reminiscent of the adage that every problem is an opportunity, but has the advantage of being a lot less trite.

The technique

An obstacle map is a simple, graphical aid to identifying the obstacles you are facing. You can reproduce the blank example below, or draw your own on a sheet of paper.

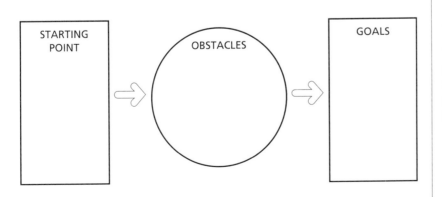

 Obstacle map

Take the first item in your diary for the next working day. Try to draw an obstacle map for whatever it covers.

In the *starting point* box, list the key aspects of the way things are now. In the *goals* box, summarize what your aims are. Now, and only now, fill in the center circle. Don't try to fix anything, just note down what stands in your way. This explicit identification of the obstacles to your success will come in very useful once you begin to work on solutions.

■ The level chain

The level chain can move you a significant distance from your starting point. It can provide extremely novel and unexpected approaches to existing situations, and is ideal for generating new product lines. In some ways it is a tougher technique than the others to get to grips with but its power makes it well worth the effort.

The technique

The level chain technique makes use of the fact mentioned at the start of this chapter that we are continually organizing, structuring and classifying the world. Everything around you fits into a vast number of different categories. If you are sitting in a chair it might fit into the category of chairs, pieces of furniture, items with four legs, things that are blue, wooden constructions, or any number of other classifications.

These classifications each occupy a "level" in our minds; the chair is at one level and the categories we listed are a level above. If the chair you are sitting in is a red chair then "red chair," which is more specific than "chair," is a level below. The level chain technique makes use of the levels which our mind creates to move up and down degrees of specificity as a way of moving away from our starting point.

Imagine that you were surveying a range of small hills before the invention of the theodolite. One approach that you could use is to stretch a very long chain from one hill to the next, to establish whether points are higher or lower than you. It is the mental version of this chain that you are using in this technique.

A quick example will make this a great deal clearer. Suppose we were looking at buttons, and wanted a more novel or exciting way of fastening clothes. The level chain process might be:

Theodolite

We originally called this the theodolite technique, but level chain seems to express the concept better. Also "theodolite" upsets spell checkers and is difficult to say.

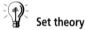

Set theory

The concept of sets – groups of objects with a common nature – has been strongly emphasized in school maths since the seventies. In our terms, a lower level object is part of the set defined by a higher level object.

> Button – (up a level to)
>
> Fastening – (down a level to)
>
> Gate latch – (up a level to)
>
> Security fixings – (down a level to)
>
> Bolts

We can stop here for some creative thought. Imagine a fashion garment which used tiny bolts instead of buttons as fastenings. This is the sort of difference that fashion designers depend on. To the best of our knowledge such fastenings do not exist, yet they could be made to be entirely practical.

The example above moved up, then down, then up, then down again. There is no need for the sequence to be this straightforward. A move up could be followed by another move up to a higher level still. Equally, a move down could be followed by another move down.

Note also that the stopping point is arbitrary – when an idea occurs. We could as easily have stopped at security fixings and decided that it would be useful to have coats with child-proof locks, to avoid small children taking them off on a cold day.

There is a tendency when using this technique to try to anticipate where you are going and then think ahead to a practical solution. This is a big mistake. The whole point of the process is that it takes you a step away from what you know is practical and allows you to see the world differently.

There is also a tendency to make sequences as neat as possible and to avoid anything remotely similar to an earlier level. We could, for instance, have moved directly from fastening to bolt in the example above. It didn't occur to us at that stage. But the fact that we had already hit upon the similar gate latch did not stop us reaching bolt later.

Before moving on to a larger example, there are a few more pointers that may be useful. The chain above is a short sequence. There is no reason whatsoever why your chains should be short. They can be as long as you find useful.

 Level chain
Put together a quick level chain looking for new products starting from the Walkman.

Neat and tidy
If a tidy desk is the sign of a tidy mind, what can an empty desk tell us?

10 minutes

The examples which we have used were generated very quickly. The level chain does not take long, but is tough to short-circuit. If you are clear about your destination you may decide to drop this technique, but if you are looking for a new goal it is irreplaceable.

TIMEOUT

The particular point which we have chosen to develop in our button example happens to be at the end of the sequence.

If nothing occurs to you, go back over the chain and be more obstinate about making relationships with your original idea. If this fails, pick a point at random in the chain and use this as the starting point for your next phase of work. It may be that you end up with a nonsensical statement such as "How to develop a tap like a policeman" but that need not matter. It could be a useful stepping stone on the way to practicality. Just for information, that statement did arise from trying to find ideas about the bathroom tap. So far we haven't taken it further but, who knows?

Example

You are the manager of a company that makes cheap fashion jewellery. Your product lines tend to be imitations of ideas generated in the more up-market end of the trade. You are keen to devote a small percentage of your production to making wholly original items of reasonably priced fashion jewellery.

Before you start you would like a theme. Starting with the concept of fashion jewellery, explore areas using the level chain to generate some original concepts which might lead to effective products.

Creativity pays off (1)

Every product you see on the shelf of the supermarket is the end result of a whole series of creative ideas. The packaging, the presentation, the contents, the attributes, all have been created. Even the idea of the shelf, at one time in the past was new, novel and entirely creative. The adaptation of our environment could not have happened in the way that it has without creative thought. Okay, enough of the history lessons. You are not interested in the historic development of mankind, you want tangible benefits for yourself.

Innovation can take three basic forms: it can involve solving a problem with an innovative solution; it can involve identifying a potential product and finding a solution which fits; it can involve having a solution and finding a problem to which it can be applied.

The humble Post-it Note is an example of a solution with no application. It was developed not because someone saw a need for sticky notes which unstuck but because 3M had accidentally developed a glue which did not dry. It was, as far as they were concerned, useless. The most popular variant of the story is that one of the developers used the glue for himself to stick paper as place markers in his hymn books. He came up with the idea of stickable notes which would unstick. The rest, as they say, is history.

■ The aerial survey

The aerial survey is a tool for viewing the environment of your problem, giving you a better understanding of its place in the world. It is an opportunity to act like a helicopter. From being stuck on the ground, wrapped up in your problem, you can now lift above the detail and take an overview. In doing this, you are trying to understand your problem in wider terms, to ensure that it is properly phrased and to gather background information which will be used throughout the Imagination Engineering process. The aerial survey is a divergent activity. You are broadening your options before narrowing down at a later stage.

The technique

The technique that we have chosen for the aerial survey is mess mapping, using mind mapping to structure and understand the mess of fact and assumption. The aerial survey will allow you to see interrelations which are not obvious to you while you are closely involved in your problem. To help associate aerial survey with this mapping technique in your mind look at the diagram overleaf; imagine yourself floating above it – taking an aerial survey.

To start drawing your aerial survey, put a description of the area you are concerned with in a box in the center of a sheet of paper. At all stages you should be using only key words, not full descriptions. Try to limit everything you put onto the survey to one or two words. With this in mind, the description in the center should be one or two words that encompass the whole area of your concern. For instance, an example below is concerned with low attendance at a concert hall. The problem statement at the center might be "Concert Attendance."

 Helicopters
Although Leonardo da Vinci is often considered to have originated the helicopter concept, it appears that the Chinese had a helicopter-like toy hundreds of years before.

 Mind mapping
Was devised by Tony Buzan. See Tony and Barry Buzan, *The Mind Map Book* (BBC Books, 1993) for a full exposition.

 Using key words
Your brain does not need complete information to understand what you have written. Keywords will use less space, be easier to see as an overview and will be far more effectively stored in the memory.

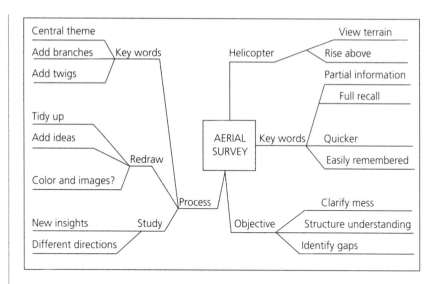

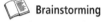

10 minutes

If you only have a short time and you find drawing a map difficult, write a short, structured list with key points and sub-points. When you are less busy, do practice drawing mind maps – they are worth the effort.

Brainstorming

For a description of brainstorming and its development see Alex F. Osborn, *Applied Imaginations: Principles and Procedures of Creative Problem Solving* (Charles Scribner's Sons, 1963).

From the central box draw a line, and put onto it a description of a subset of the area of concern or a major factor which influences it. Write the key words describing the branches and the twigs which flow out from the center, just above the lines to make a clear association between the word and the branch. From any branch many other twigs can spread as more factors and drivers occur to you. Continue to add branches as further areas come to mind; you can create new twigs which stem from the branches you have already drawn. If an area comes up which you cannot classify in your current branch structure then it is likely you need to add another branch.

The survey that you end up with will be very messy and incomplete – a partial view of the world around the problem area. If you are working on a large-scale, long-term project, now is the time to redraw it. This will allow you to smarten it up and to add further branches and twigs. At this stage you could also add color, pictures and shapes to your survey. This is a memory aid, which will help you to carry the information through your problem solving process – and it can also be fun. For a quick exercise, the original messy diagram will be fine.

There is no particular reason to perform this task on your own. Aerial surveying is a very effective group activity. Indeed, if you are about to embark on a collective attempt to solve a problem, a shared understanding of the background among the group will be more productive. Collectively drawing an aerial survey is a practical and fun way of achieving this. Traditional brainstorming can be used to gather information from the group, feeding into the diagram.

When you scan the aerial survey, you will almost certainly see that you have phrased the problem in terms of one particular branch of the survey. Look at the other branches. Will any of them allow a broader, or less obvious statement? Develop as many alternative phrasings as possible. Remember, at the moment you are broadening your options through divergent thinking. Once you have a set of possible problem statements you need to select a direction. Don't move onto this stage yet. At the end of the toolkit is a technique called "destination" which will give some tips on selecting a statement of direction.

If you are working alone on this and you are having problems redefining the problem don't be afraid to involve someone else. Explain the situation, explain the aerial survey and ask them to suggest a completely different statement of the problem which stems from it.

Example

The Muncaster Orchestra has proved a popular attraction for many years. Families often attend concerts together, and local enthusiasts are joined by visitors from miles away to listen to the orchestra play. In recent years, though, the level of attendance has been dropping. The orchestra is no longer seen as the principal attraction in the city.

Now the orchestra is close to losing money. You have been called in to help increase the level of attendance at its performances. Your brief says, "How do we get more people to visit the orchestra?", but you are aware that this may not be the most productive phrasing of the problem, and so you have decided to draw an aerial survey to give you a better understanding, and to allow you to generate different problem statements.

Take a clean sheet of paper and draw an aerial survey on concert attendance. It is likely that your survey will run through the reasons why people come to the orchestra. Also include the things that people may be doing rather than coming to a concert. Don't forget to consider alternative attractions in the town, and information about changes in lifestyles over time. There should also be an understanding of the ways the orchestra earns and spends its money.

 Destination

The section on the destination technique gives more information on selecting a problem statement – see Destination, p. 38.

 Aerial survey

Take three minutes to survey your number one problem of the moment.

 Delphic oracle

Don't worry if you don't know much about orchestras. A popular forecasting technique, Delphi, depends on feeding back the opinions of a group to themselves and refining those results. Often there is no benefit from intimate knowledge of the field. So, launch out in a Delphi coracle.

 Delphi

An excellent story of a world run by the Delphi technique is John Brunner's *The Shockwave Rider* (Quartet, 1975).

How to ...

The "How to ..." question is taken directly from the work of Tudor Rickards, professor at Manchester Business School, where creativity training has been run since 1972. It is used because it is less clumsy than the "In what way might" question of Arthur Vangundy.

Contradictions

Points 5 and 6 appear contradictory. In creative problem solving, apparent contradictions are essential. Despite the superficial conflict, these statements are complementary.

10 minutes

Even if you only have 10 minutes, you must write out a problem statement, and it would be most effective if it measured well against the checklist. Try the exercise.

Once you have the survey drawn as fully as you want, look at the alternatives it suggests. List as many different phrasings of the problem as you can in a minute or two. Stop at this point. A large list of poorly structured phrasings of a problem is not as useful as one well formulated problem statement, but having a list from which to select is a significant step forward. The final surveying tool, destination, will help with clarification of your problem statements.

■ The destination

This whole chapter is based on the premise that a clear statement of your problem is an important first stage in the process of finding a solution. Much of what we have covered is concerned with understanding the world, either through making sense of the mess, or through finding broad directions in which we need to move. The destination technique involves stating the problem in the most fruitful way (or ways) to allow us to move on.

The technique

The technique itself is simply to develop a clear question or a series of questions starting with the words "How to ..." and then state the direction we wish to follow. In some ways this is not so much a technique as a process with guidelines which give a more effective result if they are followed than if they are not.

The list of guidelines below are heavily adapted from Vangundy and other authors.

1 Be concise.
2 Be silly or trivial if you want.
3 Be productive – generate lots of problem statements.
4 Be active – make your statements action oriented.
5 Be precise – include one problem in each statement.
6 Be vague – don't include precise measures in your statements (they tend to channel thought).
7 Be prepared to spend time – use the survey techniques to generate your problem statements.

In short, write out your problem in the form, "How to ...?" followed by a punchy, action-focussed statement. Write out different manifestations of the problem. If you have time to generate solutions to more than one problem statement, select as many as you feel you can handle. If you have time for only one, that's fine. Make sure that you are not choosing statements because they are the ones you are most comfortable with. These will tend to portray the world in the way you see it already, and so will be the least challenging.

Example

If you have been through the exercises presented so far in this chapter you can provide your own material for practicing this technique. Look at your earlier results, particularly anywhere you generated a large number of alternative phrasings, and develop at least one really good statement of direction. This is your destination for the surveying phase of the Imagination Engineering process. When you have produced it, measure it against the checklist of criteria for good problem statements above. If you feel that it could be improved, spend a little time on improving it. If it meets all of the criteria then give yourself a pat on the back and prepare to move on to the next stage.

No destination

Once you have a clear destination, make sure that you really want to go there. It is particularly necessary where the problem is a personal one such as being overweight. It might be that we are going through the motions of finding a solution but we are doing this because we believe it is expected of us, not because we have a real commitment to solving the problem. The final aspect of the destination technique is about asking whether this is really a problem for us or whether we have defined it as a problem in order to meet the expectations of others.

How bad is our world if there is no way to reach the destination we have set ourselves? Are there ways that we can learn to live with the problems caused? Is, in fact, the effort of putting a solution in place more expensive than the downsides of the problem?

We should also ask what benefits does this problem have for us? This sounds a bizarre question but bear in mind that you may be contributing to the continuation of the problem and to be doing this, there are likely to be some benefits in it for you.

Speed writing
Prove to yourself how little time it takes to use the destination technique. Pick a real problem you have dealt with and spend 3 minutes (no more) writing as many different "How to" statements as you can.

Edward de Bono

A major contributor to the field of creativity. The author of the book (and the term) Lateral Thinking, and developer of a plethora of thinking techniques.

If you still see this as a problem worth investing energy in solving then the chances are that you should stick with the destination you have. If you find that you are no longer sure that this is something you are going to really work at changing, then alarm bells should be ringing. Remember, it usually takes some effort to solve a problem. There are certainly problems which go away of their own accord but if this one won't, then it will take a piece of you to solve it. Are you willing to put that piece of you into the game?

 **TIMEOUT**

Ha Ha!

A sandwich walked into a bar and the barman said, "Get out! We don't serve food in here." Or, even more directly – a man walked into a bar and said, "Ouch!" It was an iron bar.

All right, so they're not funny, but they illustrate the point. Most humor is based on an unexpected twist in meaning. The first of these makes use of the double meaning inherent in the word, "serve," the second makes use of the double meaning inherent in the word "bar." Some humor is pun based as these are, some is based on challenging an assumption which we have made in the hearing of the story. Usually short punchy jokes are pun based and it takes longer jokes to challenge assumptions. A master of the short, challenging joke is Stephen Wright, a beautifully understated American comedian famous for short, weird, one liners such as, "I lost a button hole today." or , "I bought some batteries... but they weren't included... so I had to buy them again ..."

Humor is of fundamental importance to creativity. With due respect to Edward de Bono's view in *Serious Creativity* (Harper Collins, 1993), it is awfully hard to be seriously creative. De Bono argues that it's not enough *just* to have fun – quite right. But there's no reason why you can't use serious techniques in an enjoyable way. It is necessary to take humor and having fun in creativity seriously, but certainly not necessary to be dour. One reason why you will find so many ideas from Roger von Oech spreading around the place is that his books are fun, his style is light but his techniques still work. The creative process is inherently enjoyable. It is probable that the better you get at it, the more fun you will have from it.

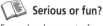 **Serious or fun?**

For a development of de Bono's argument that creativity shouldn't be fun, see *Journal for Quality and Participation* (September 1995), pp. 12–17.

HOW TO PUT IT TOGETHER

Roger von Oech
A creativity guru based in California whose light style has made him popular with Silicon Valley.

The toolkit you have looked at is only the start. With experience, you will get a feel for when it's right to spend more time on a survey or the compass and when you should rush through to the destination.

If you are coming fresh to a problem area it is always worth conducting an aerial survey. Indeed, even trying to get a fresh look at an old problem will make this worthwhile. If you are trying to alter your perspective on a problem use the compass. If you are trying to move away from your starting point to get a radically new view, use the level chain. As the last stage of the surveying process, always state your destination.

Coming soon ➤➤➤

Once you have stated your destination, it is time to move on from surveying to the next of the four stages of the Imagination Engineering framework – building. Here the full weight of creativity techniques will be brought into play in order to reach your destination despite obstacles and uncertainty.

Key words
Destination; compass; level chain; obstacle map; aerial survey.

TALE PIECE

THE CHANNEL

By Brian Clegg

The first thing she noticed when the strong-sprung door had snapped shut behind her was the organ, playing something strange that managed to be harmonious and dissonant at the same time. That was before she was aware of the shafts of light from the high clerestory windows, dust mote sanctuaries every one, and before the rich, heavy, decadent scent of incense touched her consciousness. She tried to find a tune in the tangled skein of notes, but each time she felt that she had grasped a thread, something new came through.

A choir joined in now, unison men with solemn, pure voices that sent a shiver down her spine. Morwenna hesitated. Perhaps there was a service taking place. Maybe she should not be there. High boys' voices soared over the men for a second or two, but faltered, interrupted by three firm handclaps and a buzz of distant, commanding speech. It was a practice, then. No need for concern. Now she relaxed enough to let the rest of her senses function, to take in the size and emptiness and light of the building. And to let her desperation slip back into place, no longer held off by the panic of intrusion.

She forced herself to walk down the gravestone-carpeted aisle, skirting the nave, catching flickering glimpses of ornate, carved monuments without stopping to read them. Now she heard another voice, cutting flatly across the re-started strands of music; a heavy, dull, man's voice that came from the stone filigree curtain screening her from the back of the soaring pulpit.

"Notice," said the voice with pompous self-importance, "notice the little stone channel running up from this ornately decorated cavity to the back of the pulpit, emerging by the preacher's head. What do you think that might be?"

Morwenna craned to see who was speaking, who his audience was. She could see tiny patches of moving color through the screen, but no detail.

"Is it a drain?" said a small voice, a child, eager with the intensity of youth. Where does the enthusiasm go? thought Morwenna. Why don't we stay interested and hopeful?

"It's not a drain," said the flat voice, "but that's very good, it might well have been. No, you see, this cavity down below used to contain the relic of a saint – that would be his or her finger or some such thing, preserved in a jewelled casket." There were sharp intakes of breath from his young audience, though whether from awe at the thought of the dismembered saint, or consideration of the jewelled casket, it was not clear. "Now the medieval masons who built this cathedral believed that they could channel the power from that relic through the stone. That the stone conduit would lead holiness to the speaker and inspire his words. That's what it was for."

Clerestory

An upper row of windows in a cathedral or large church, above the level of the aisle roofs (*Concise Oxford Dictionary*, OUP).

Morwenna moved on, padding alone around the back of the sanctuary, past the Lady Chapel, circling the drifting voices of the choir – now quiet, now harsh. It was there, all alone but for the music, that she saw the hunched figure. It was a woman, about her own age. She was on the floor, nestling in the space between a huge wooden chest and an incongruously modern pile of scaffolding. Another down-and-out, she supposed, another discard of humanity. She remembered some long dead homily about there always being someone worse off than yourself. "Stupid," said Morwenna, not realizing that she had spoken out loud until the echoes came back to her.

It was stupid, though. She, Morwenna, had no purpose, nothing of value, only money and security. The woman on the floor might be destitute, but she must have something to drive her, something to aim for, or surely she would not still be alive. That was how Morwenna saw it. She took a few steps closer, examining the figure in detail as if she was an interesting facet of the building. Her hair was past the shoulder, like Morwenna's own, though it was not possible to say quite how long it was because she lay on it. There was a welcome familiarity about the face, too. No doubt she resembled some TV personality.

Morwenna coughed, at first gently, then louder. Her faint curiosity transformed into concern. There was no movement, no movement at all from the woman. Perhaps she was on drugs, Morwenna thought. Perhaps she was unwell. She reached forward and touched the woman's shoulder. It shifted easily, like a piece of meat on the butcher's slab and now, only now when she was close enough to touch, did Morwenna's eyes light on the wrists, running with a dark red stream of lifeblood.

"Oh shit!" Morwenna said. She slapped the woman's face. "Wake up!" There was no response. What did you do when someone cut their wrists? Surely not artificial respiration. Morwenna had always resisted first aid classes; she was squeamish, it wasn't for her.

She jumped up and ran round into the nave. There was nobody there. The whole, great church was an empty shell, an uninhabited stone cave. A scraping from the choir area drew her attention. At least she knew there was someone there. She ran back up the aisle, passing the body (was it a body if it wasn't yet dead?), slipping on the polished stone as she turned sharp right into the chancel.

For the first time she saw the choir. They were ranged out in the high, decorated stalls, not, as she had expected, decked in bright colored robes and swirling white surplices, but wearing everyday clothes: jeans and cords, T-shirts and polo shirts. The choirmaster stood close by, hunched over his music desk like a caricature vulture. "That's not it at all," he said. His voice was as fruity as the guide's had been flat. "This is Howells, not Bach. You can't count it strictly, I want it to flow, to pluck the heartstrings. From the top of page three." He raised his hand. Morwenna knew that she could not

Herbert Howells (1892–1983)
Organist and composer, best known for his striking and passionate church music.

bring herself to interrupt the whole choir, not insignificant Morwenna. Even here, trying to save a life, she was unimportant.

The choirmaster brought down his right hand as Morwenna thought this, holding the choir back with his left, moving them along, almost physically pushing them through the lyrical line. His body swayed from side to side as the music danced in a triplet of jazz-like notes.

Morwenna bit her lip. Where else? There must be someone else in a place the size of this. There must be someone without the armor of responsibility and music. She clattered across to the far side of the chancel, out into the South aisle. The shop. She had seen a sign to the shop in the South transept; there must be someone in the shop.

There was. No customers, but a comfortable, grey-haired woman. Not old, not really old, in her fifties perhaps. She had big, brown eyes that made Morwenna think of Bambi. "Help me," said Morwenna. That sounded pathetic, she knew, but it was hard to think what else to say. "I've found someone who's hurt herself. Cut her wrists. Please come."

The woman looked concerned. Mrs Rigden, she was called; it said so on her name badge. "I'm sorry, dear," she said, "I shouldn't leave the shop unattended."

"She could be dead!"

"Don't say that," said Mrs Rigden, "not dead." She came to a decision, turning a key in the big, old fashioned cash register and slipping it into the pocket of the apron she wore over a navy dress. "Let's have a look," she said. "I can shut for a moment. We aren't overburdened with visitors this afternoon."

"Come quickly," said Morwenna, dancing around like a small child waiting to visit the tree on Christmas Day.

"Yes, yes, I'm coming." Mrs Rigden pulled shut the modern, oak door of the shop and locked it with a key from the big chain at her waist. "Where is she?"

"This way." Morwenna took Mrs Rigden's wrist for a moment, but only a moment, releasing it, not wanting to seem too familiar. She hurried across the cathedral, cutting through the chancel, always looking back to see if Mrs Rigden was with her. Right then, as she crossed, she didn't notice that anything was different, although it was.

The niche by the scaffolding seemed darker now, so dark that Morwenna had to look twice to convince herself that there was nothing there. Nothing at all. No body, not even a rag that she could have convinced herself was a corpse. "It was here," she said, realizing how stupid, how unbelievable she sounded. "It really was here."

She expected Mrs Rigden to go away, to look at Morwenna strangely and to hurry off, but instead she smiled. "It's easy to be fooled by the light in this place, especially when you're under a strain. Now I've closed up I might as well have my break – would you like a cup of tea? You can tell me about your problems, if it'll help at all."

"Thank you," said Morwenna. She hadn't realized she was quite so transparent, that the despair showed in her face, even her stance. She followed meekly behind Mrs Rigden, happy to give responsibility to someone else. They passed through the chancel and only now did she notice what had changed. The choir was not there. There was only an American couple, admiring the carving on the reredos. "They must have hurried away very quickly," she said, wanting to make conversation so as not to seem too burdensome.

"Who's that?" said Mrs Rigden.

"The choir. They were practicing only a minute ago."

"Oh, no, you've got that wrong. The choir won't be practicing until four o'clock. It's always four o'clock on a weekday."

Morwenna stopped in the vaulted aisle. "I did see them; they were here." And though she had persuaded herself that the body had been an illusion, she knew again that she had touched it; she had felt the cool flesh.

"Come and have a cup of tea," said Mrs Rigden, only now she seemed less motherly and more covetous, as if she had some motive for getting Morwenna away.

"No!" screamed Morwenna. She shook off the woman's hand and pelted down the aisle towards the great West door, running, sobbing, full of her own sorrow. She was half way along the nave when she saw the coffin. She stopped suddenly, horrified, wondering what they must think. The funeral procession was proceeding down the center of the church at a snail's pace. Step and halt. Step and halt. They didn't look towards her, but they must have heard, must have been disturbed by the noise she had made.

She tried to put herself in their place, but the only funeral she had ever been to was her Gran's and that was at the crematorium with no such ornate formality. In fact, when the coffin had started moving on its own and the curtains had drawn themselves across, Morwenna had felt she was an extra in a rather sick comedy show. She couldn't imagine how they felt. So bleak, so ... funereal they looked. All dressed in black. The odd thing was the kitten on the coffin. Amid all the black there was a shiny gold kitten, riding the box high on the pallbearers' shoulders. Fancifully, she imagined that the girl she had found, Morwenna's disappearing body, was in the coffin. But that couldn't be; funerals didn't happen just like that.

Morwenna turned away and tiptoed towards the door, straining her legs to avoid putting her shoes down with a click. If they had heard, they would forget her soon enough. She reached the door, turning to look after the procession, but it was already out of sight behind the screen. As she turned back she stepped straight into something bulky and black. It gave a little and smelled of mothballs.

"Mind where you're going," said a droning voice. It was the guide, the same one she had heard earlier. He wore a black gown of office and a smug expression.

"I'm sorry," said Morwenna. "I didn't realize there was a funeral on. I didn't see any notices."

"What funeral?" said the guide.

"Just then, they went up the aisle," said Morwenna. "I passed them coming down."

"The nave," said the guide pedantically. "The aisles are at the side; it's the nave in the middle."

"The nave, then. You must have seen them. A big, black coffin with a gold cat on top."

"Very funny," said the guide. "Most amusing. And I fell for it, for a moment at least. It's for a bet is it? Little game with your friends?"

"What do you mean?"

"There's only been one funeral here with a cat on the coffin. Lucy Barr in 1867. I suppose you saw the engraving in the guide book. Very droll."

"I don't understand."

"That's both of us, then," said the guide. "Go on, now, go away and stop bothering me."

This isn't real, thought Morwenna, walking slowly back to where she had found the body. It's like a play; who was it wrote those plays about time? "An Inspector Calls" and all that. Was it the same as "Murder in the Cathedral?" That would be apt. But no, that was Eliot and the time plays were by someone different. Time here seemed to be out of control, to be moving at different speeds through the stone vastness. She thought of the guide's talk, the channel for the essence of the relics. Why not a channel for time?

She had reached the spot now. A knife was perched on the edge of the scaffolding pile. It had been there before she thought. Perhaps. She picked it up, feeling the heavy weight of the metal in her hands. Why not a stone channel for time? She sat in the narrow gap between the chest and the scaffolding. Why not? She was unhappy, was never going to recover her happiness. Why not complete the chain and prove that the cathedral controlled time?

She let the knife blade rest against her wrist, feeling the cold pressure of the steel on her skin. It did not hurt. It wasn't even cutting, wouldn't until she drew it across. She could imagine the way it would scrape, the flow of blood. Inside her something swelled, a claustrophobic panic. She didn't want to be trapped, didn't want to fit into the building's tortuous pattern. The knife clattered as it hit the floor and again her footsteps were rattling on the pavement of gravestones, only this time nothing stopped her, nothing kept her from pulling at the quaint door handle and emerging, blinking, into the moving, noisy, ordinary-time, air.

 Time in fiction
She was thinking of J.B. Priestley. The treatment of time in fiction ranges from H.G. Wells' mechanistic time machine to the many science fiction views of the paradoxes arising from travelling back in time and changing the present.

She ran on a few more paces and stopped, looking back at the huge, enigmatic face of the cathedral, turning its empty gaze upon her. The three, high door arches were eyes and mouths at the same time. It had waited; it could wait. She would return. Carried on some errant breeze, she could hear the organ launch once more into the anguished harmony of Howells.

Key thoughts

- Time is often a constraint to our thinking. What would happen to your problem if time flowed backwards?
- Music can often inspire a different track of thought
- Cause and effect are not always clearly differentiated.

BUILDING

IMAGINATION ENGINEERING

 Bore, n. A person who talks when you wish him to listen. (*The Enlarged Devil's Dictionary*, Ambrose Bierce).

Bore Make hole in, usu. with revolving tool, hollow out evenly (tube etc.)
(*The Concise Oxford Dictionary*, OUP).

Fixed pathways
See Timeout – Creativity blockers – you, p. 81.

The unorthodox engineers
Appeared in a number of 1960s stories by Colin Kapp. Collected in the "*New Writings in SF*" volumes, but rarely seen today. The engineers solved apparently impossible engineering problems (such as a planet where the gravity constantly changed, or a subway system that seemed designed to kill its passengers) with very creative solutions.

UNCIVIL ENGINEERING

In our local Yellow Pages if you look up Boring you will find "See Civil Engineers." This is obviously a disgraceful slur on civil engineers who may well be extremely interesting people. The building process we are looking at here is described as "Uncivil Engineering" in part because it is anything but boring.

Building involves creating something new from a collection of raw materials. The raw materials you are working with in Imagination Engineering are your thoughts, memories, ideas and, underlying them all, your brain's ability to link them together. This linking process normally develops fixed pathways which are useful – even essential – to your life. It can be, though, that the same linkages get in the way when you want to move away from the paths you normally follow into more creative territory. The techniques which we cover in this chapter allow you to shift beyond the links which your brain normally makes, into new territories. Some of the techniques will nudge you gently out of your accustomed paths, others will kick much harder.

You want to travel from A to B, seemingly a simple proposition. But there is an obstacle in the way. Sometimes this obstacle is self-created; your brain, by working in its accustomed paths, makes B appear to be an impossible goal even when it is not. Sometimes the obstacle is real and creative thinking is needed to find a route around it.

Given this picture of a route and an obstacle, it should be no surprise to learn that the techniques we use in the building process fit into categories which allow you to tunnel under obstacles, bridge over them, create a by-pass around them or even to find a new destination. It is important to stress that these are mostly not *our* techniques. We have borrowed from and adapted the work of a whole range of writers in the field of creativity.

Wherever possible we have pointed you to appropriate sources in the book references in the margins. It is often difficult to credit an original source because so many of the ideas here have been developing for decades. Arthur Koestler and Alex Osborn could be regarded as the early developers of many of the principles on which

50

the creativity techniques we employ are based, but even they were building on the work of earlier thinkers.

It is instructive to look at the creativity techniques in use today as

Self-patterning systems

De Bono and others have described the brain as a self-patterning system, rather like a tray of wax into which a hot liquid is gently poured. As you pour, the liquid will begin to melt channels in the wax. Over time these channels will become reinforced by more hot liquid and will become deeper ruts. Our brains create similar ruts. We need tools to help us to leap out of them into the surrounding high ground.

problem solving tools and ask how many of them stem from Osborn's original list:

- Questions – What other uses? What uses as is?
- Adaption, modification, substitution
- Addition, multiplication, subtraction, division
- Rearrangement, reversal, combination

In our view, many of the techniques we use have their origins in this list. Since Osborn's work there has been a whole generation of experience in the use of these techniques, new methods have been developed, and new ways of using the old faithfuls have evolved. Yet there is still an obvious debt to earlier thinkers in all modern work on creative problem solving.

The Imagination Engineering analogy is very strong in this chapter but it can be hard to associate each of the techniques with their relevant mapping counterparts. It is valuable to work at this because a strong link formed now will make the tools more accessible and more available later. It is not uncommon for people trained in creativity techniques, even some of those who sell their expertise to others, to rely on one or two techniques even though they may have become stale with repetition. The thinking behind Imagination Engineering is that you will have a broader kit of tools readily available to you and that this kit will allow you to use the right tool for the right job.

"People who are only good with hammers see every problem as a nail." (Abraham Maslow)

"And it ought to be remembered that there is nothing more difficult to take in hand, more perilous to conduct, or more uncertain in its success, than to take the lead in the introduction of a new order of things. Because the innovator has for enemies all those who have done well under the old conditions, and lukewarm defenders in those who may do well under the new." (Niccolo Machiavelli, *The Prince* (1515)).

Before getting into the tools it is worth highlighting that the way that you use these tools is critical to their success. A major obstacle that you face in being creative is the reaction of other people around you. Underestimating the power of the negative comments of your colleagues could be the undoing of a good idea. The chapter on way-marking will help with this, but at this stage think through the possible reaction to the way you are developing your ideas. Who do you need to include in the development process? How will they react to the techniques you have at your disposal? How will your attitude and demeanor affect the acceptance of the technique you want to use? It is our experience that you can achieve an incredible amount with chutzpah. Act as though you've done this a hundred times before, believe in yourself, explain the background to what you are doing and even the most pessimistic will go along with you.

 **TIMEOUT**

Creativity pays off (2)

Creativity is often more about working at finding a solution than waiting for a bolt from the blue. Much new product development falls into this category. The developer has a field in which a new market niche exists or a market which is demanding improvement and they develop a product to fit. As I write this I am listening to a compact disc of Cajun music (there's no accounting for taste). The CD is the latest step in the search for ever better ways of perfectly reproducing sound. There will be others. There will also be developments in the areas of portability of equipment. There will no doubt be developments, which integrate entertainment and communications, such that I do not have to have purchased this disc to listen to it. I could download the ability to listen from a central source and pay for each usage rather than paying to own a disc. There is a thin line between these potential applications and problems. It could be argued that the list of potential developments above represents minor problems in the current method of listening to reproduced sound.

Most innovations and creative solutions, however, start life as clear problems. We are faced with a large gap between the way we want the world to be and the way it is. The creative solution is the route over, around or through that gap. An example which we particularly like was the search for a machine which could pick tomatoes. For centuries automation had been improving the cultivation of farm produce and yet a mechanical tomato picker proved elusive. The skins of tomatoes were too tender and any mechanical device which could hold hard enough to pick them would also hold hard enough to damage them. While this search was going on someone turned the problem on its head and asked how to make a tomato tough enough to withstand picking (for the sake of the story we wish we could tell you who but we just don't know). The result is the tougher skinned tomato which is now commonplace.

BUILDING TOOLKIT

This is the point where we move on to the heart of creativity: tools which help you to see the world in a different way. There are those who say that you do not need a toolkit and that you need only develop your ability to think. Our contention is that developing your ability to think is only a less obvious way of developing a mental toolkit, and that making the tools explicit gives you a far higher chance of success than hoping that you will absorb their effects by some form of osmosis.

The process is a little like the development of a master artist. People who know little of the creative process might argue that because Picasso was a master and demonstrated his mastery by developing whole new ways of representing the world, one can similarly become a master merely by breaking the rules. In Picasso's case he was a master artist before he developed new forms of representation. The mistake of much of the pop art of the last few decades has been to have an idea for a new representation without the skill necessary to make it real. Art is having the vision to see the world differently and the skill to portray that vision. Having skill without seeing the world differently is the basis of craftsmanship. Having no skill and a novel view of the world is the source of much frustration. Our intention is to develop your skill in creativity in order to allow you to become an artist.

The toolkit is divided into tunneling tools, bridging tools, by-passing tools and tools for developing a new destination altogether. The distinctions between these categories are quite fuzzy. We have made them in order to break down the techniques into more manageable chunks. We said earlier that you remember more effectively if you

Techniques

We have chosen a small selection of creativity techniques within this book. For a glimpse at the breadth available see James M. Higgins', *101 Creative Problem Solving Techniques*, (New Management Publishing, 1994) or Brian Clegg and Paul Birch's *Instant Creativity* (Kogan Page, 1999).

Memory

A classic book on memory techniques is Harry Lorayne's, *Secrets of Mind Power* (A Thomas & Co., 1963). For a more recent view, try Alan Baddeley, *Your Memory – A User's Guide* (Penguin, 1994) or Brian Clegg, *Instant Brainpower* (Kogan Page, 1999).

develop strong, concrete associations with something which is intangible. You also remember more effectively if the things you are remembering are arranged in certain groups. You can remember 27 items far more easily if they are structured into a sensible hierarchy which has three branches each dividing into three and then into three again than if they are structured as a straight list of 27.

As an example, read and remember this list of objects:

cat, shark, hawk, oak, rose, mushroom, table, television, door, dog, stingray, eagle, birch, dandelion, toadstool, chair, hi-fi, window, chimpanzee, goldfish, sparrow, beech, lavender, puff ball, desk, kettle, radiator.

Now here is the same list in a more structured form:

ANIMALS

Mammals	Fish	Birds
cat	shark	hawk
dog	stingray	eagle
chimpanzee	goldfish	sparrow

PLANTS

Trees	Flowers	Fungi
oak	rose	mushroom
birch	dandelion	toadstool
beech	lavender	puff ball

HOUSEHOLD OBJECTS

Furniture	Electrical goods	Fixtures
table	television	door
chair	hi-fi	window
desk	kettle	radiator.

For most people it is far easier to recall the second, structured list than the first, disordered one. We hope to provide that same ease of recall with the Imagination Engineering structure.

So remember, we are going to introduce you to chunks of techniques divided into tunneling tools, bridging tools, by-passing tools and tools for developing a new destination.

■ Tunnel

- *Challenging an assumption*
- *Distortion*
- *Reversal*

The tunnel is a way of defeating an obstacle by making the obstacle invisible to us. When you are travelling through a tunnel you cannot see the tower blocks and streets of the city over your head. They are there and they were a consideration to the person who built the route you are travelling on, but they need not bother you once the tunnel is built.

We have chosen three techniques of tunneling under obstacles. "Challenge a given assumption" denies the most basic aspects of the problem. "Distortion" changes the magnitude of the problem, making it much larger or smaller. "Reversal" makes the opposite of your scenario true and deals with that as a problem. Don't worry that these explanations seem silly: the techniques themselves are not. You will understand, once you start to use them, that they provide a powerful mechanism for building a tunnel under the obstacles you face and allow you to reach your destination.

These techniques have been grouped together as tunneling techniques because they all burrow into the assumptions which underlie a problem or the world surrounding the problem.

 Tunnels
The Simplon Tunnel between Italy and Switzerland, built around the turn of the century, was for many years the world's longest railroad tunnel and forms part of the route of the Orient Express.

 Silly
Foolish, imprudent, unwise ... (*Concise Oxford Dictionary*, OUP). But wisdom is based on exactly the well-trodden tracks that we are trying to break away from.

 TIMEOUT

Galileo Galilei

An extreme example of an organization's willingness to close its eyes to evidence is the story of Galileo. In this case the "organization" was the whole of society, particularly educational and religious leaders.

In 1609 Galileo built a telescope capable of twenty times magnification. With this he was able to observe the mountains of the Moon, some of the moons of Jupiter, the individual stars which made up the Milky Way. He managed to collect evidence which demonstrated that the Earth circled the Sun.

His beliefs were held to be heretical. Galileo argued that he could prove the truth of his propositions by showing the way that Venus behaved through his telescope (at the time Venus was widely thought to

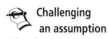

Challenging an assumption

What does your business do? Assume you wanted to grow your business – how would you do it in a world where your prime activity was suddenly made illegal? Now turn it around: could variants on your idea be used in today's world? Often they can.

be two stars, one of which appeared in the morning and one in the evening). The authorities refused to look through the telescope. Their argument was that the scriptures (and their interpretation of the scriptures) defined truth and that human senses were less reliable.

In 1633 he was found guilty of heresy and sentenced to life imprisonment. This sentence was commuted to lifelong house arrest. Just to prove that organizations do adapt over time (approximately 350 years), in 1984 a Papal commission acknowledged that the church had been wrong.

Challenge a given assumption

Given that creativity techniques can be thought of as a way of breaking out of our restraints, this one is a must. The technique asks you to challenge the most basic assumption you have about the problem at hand. It's rather like having the problem of disguising a huge boil on the end of your nose and starting with the assumption that the boil does not exist. Ask yourself what would you do to enhance your appearance under these circumstances. The chances are that some of your ideas would be very effective, but had been dismissed because the huge boil was so coloring your opinion that you could not see their value. Some may even distract from the blemish.

As an example, let's say you wanted to improve the work of a firm of lawyers – then start with the assumption that they know nothing about the law. How would they work? Who would buy anything from them? Who could they represent and how? What would they have to improve in order to make money if this situation continued?

The notion itself is simple but the reasoning behind it might need a little explanation. Why would you want to ignore the most basic premise about a problem when that premise is a given? Why even bother wasting your time thinking about lawyers who know nothing about the law when this is the main skill which they trade on? The answer is that you will automatically have covered ideas about how to trade on their skill as lawyers. This is the thinking which will generate the obvious, easy to do ideas which are, frankly, rather dull. If you are looking for something more novel and appealing then this technique could help.

Lawyers

"The first thing we do, let's kill all the lawyers." (William Shakespeare, *King Henry VI Part II*)

In practice lawyers trade on far more than their skill at law. Thinking about how you would convince someone to hire a lawyer who knew nothing about the law will introduce you to a whole host of areas which you will have to develop anyway in order to be a successful law firm.

The sorts of questions this technique will raise are: How to advertise? How to make the offices look appealing? How to develop unbeatable customer service? How to demonstrate a track record of success when the lawyer is actually useless? How to develop other businesses? How to find a partner who is a legal hot shot? How to get very good at the non-legal aspects of the profession and then sell your services to other law firms? You can see that there is actually a great deal to think about beyond the obvious, basic element of the business.

This technique works well for other areas beyond legal firms. It is most useful when dealing with product and service development but it can be used with just about any problem as a means of shifting the focus away from the areas which are already mined out to new, fruitful seams.

Distortion – change the size of the problem

This technique was one of the earliest ones used when creative problem solving was developing as a field of study. It simply involves distorting what you know about a critical part of your problem. You can make it larger. You can make it smaller. You can have an abundance of something which you know is in short supply. You can have few of something you know is extremely common. Something which blends into the background can be made to jump out and proclaim itself. Something which is obvious can be hidden. Whatever distortion you make must alter the scale and complexity of the problem.

As an example, imagine you are faced with the task of improving your company's public relations. Inevitably you would consider the number of people with whom you must communicate.

As a distortion, what if your own link with your customers was through advertising in a single magazine? How would you manage to communicate with your customers? Develop a plan for getting information to them and opinions back from them. Now, how could

 Do it

Do try working through your own example of these exercises. Whilst reading a book can be informative, it is far better to try doing it for yourself.

Buying the channel

In their UK launch of Windows 95, Microsoft bought a whole day's print run of *The Times* newspaper, giving it away. While the stunt brought lots of publicity, it is uncertain that the newspaper reached the audience Microsoft intended.

you adapt the ways you used this single channel to the real requirements of a large company? Perhaps the magazine is such an important vehicle of communication that you should buy it outright. Would this limited channel influence you to have in-house P.R. people, or use an agency? If you thought of buying the magazine, should you produce your own magazine? What would induce the customers to read it?

Alternatively, what if your company dealt through every single publication in the country from newspapers to children's comics? What would be the advantages and disadvantages of this approach? How would you tailor the message to the different publications? How would you deal with the different journalists? What campaigns could you run in a woman's magazine or a magazine for railway enthusiasts? Having developed ideas for this distorted problem, how can you adapt them to cope with the size of your company?

In many ways this is a quick and easy technique. It is certainly one which you can use effectively on your own or in a group session. Quick and easy does not, however, mean that it is lightweight. It is effective and powerful. Try it on a real problem; you may be surprised.

TIMEOUT

Failure – Feynman

Richard Feynman, 1965 Nobel prize winner for physics and modern polymath, said that, "To develop working ideas efficiently, I try to fail as fast as I can." Indeed, his stories are often a testament to the power of failure. Most of us explain how we have achieved something through a post hoc rationalization process which starts with the end point and works backwards. Often reality doesn't work this way. In telling our stories as success stories in which we set out to achieve the end result we reinforce the view that failure is wrong.

Reversal

The reversal technique is also a tool which allows you to tunnel under obstacles. In fact it is an exaggerated case of distortion, where the problem becomes so distorted that you turn it inside-out.

Using the previous example of improving public relations, the reversal technique would have you asking how you can completely prevent any form of communication with the public. What can you do to destroy any chance of anyone knowing what is happening? What can you do to prevent them letting you know what they feel or giving you ideas? The most depressing thing about this technique is that it takes very little time to discover that you are already doing some of the things that effectively prevent communication with your customers.

The final stage of generating ideas using this technique is, obviously, to work them into their opposites. In other words, having developed ways of preventing communication, how can you take these and treat them as obstacles to be removed? How can you prevent these obstacles developing?

This technique is particularly effective at helping with problems which appear massive and insurmountable. It is often the case that the biggest problems are the ones where we are the largest obstacle. Playing with the reversal technique makes apparent the things that we are doing which stand in the way of success.

■ Bridge

- *Fantasy*
- *Someone else's problem*
- *It's just like …*

The bridging techniques are more insubstantial than the tunneling techniques. They are less focussed on the underlying assumptions; they involve floating above the problem and seeing it from a higher viewpoint. They all make use of story telling, characterization, analogy or metaphor, in some way.

Building the bridge involves a greater separation from the problem than the tunneling techniques. You travel a long way above before coming back down to earth again. There are three bridging techniques laid out below: fantasy, someone else's problem and it's just like …

Tunneling
- Challenging an assumption
- Distortion
- Reversal.

Bridges
The Tacoma Narrows Bridge, affectionately known as Galloping Gertie, claimed a place in history by being filmed dramatically flexing into pieces within months of opening in 1940.

TIMEOUT

Creativity blockers

An excellent description of creativity blockers can be found in Roger von Oech's, *A Whack on the Side of the Head* (Warner, 1983).

Creativity blockers – the brain

We tend to talk about the brain in the singular (see, we just did), but in fact it has two distinct halves which are linked by a thick bundle of nerves called the corpus callosum. These halves often work together to allow you to think but they have different strengths. They get more involved in some activities than others. The left side of your brain deals with logical, sequential thought. It deals with speech and with numbers. It deals with elements and sub-divisions. The right side of your brain is more holistic. It deals with imagery and color. It deals with the whole tune, not the individual notes or the structure of the music.

Many people believe that the right half of the brain is more creative than the left. This is not necessarily true. The problem which most of us face is that in our training and development through school and in society we have been taught to focus on using the left side of the brain and to exclude the right. Logic and erudition are valued more than effective use of color or imagery. The right and left halves of the brain are both essential to creative thought but we need to focus especially on the right half because we are already very good at using the left. This is the reason why many of the zanier creativity techniques use imagery, color and music. They are working at stimulating the right hand side of the brain.

The dominance of the left is also one of the reasons why creativity gets killed quickly if there is no structure in which to nurture it. The left hand side of the brain is naturally evaluative. As soon as an idea starts to form, your left brain will be leaping in and saying why it may, or (more often) may not, work. Most structured creativity techniques are ways of making use of both halves of the brain at the correct stage in the process. There is a time to evaluate ideas but they need a chance to grow a few leaves before we try to prune them.

Recent thinking has called the left/right brain split into question as being too simplistic, but it doesn't really matter if the physical cause is correct: the outcome is observably true.

Fantasy

Daydreaming is a skill we lose as we go through life. We are actively discouraged from daydreaming at school (in Paul's case, very actively discouraged!). We are taught as we travel through our lives that we should be focussed, professional, and determined, avoiding the temptation to drift off into impossible dreams. Forget all of that teaching. Daydreaming is a skill which you need to rediscover in yourself. For some particularly bloody-minded individuals this may be a skill which they have clung onto despite all of the pressures to lose it. For others the rediscovery will take some effort.

The basis of the fantasy technique is to say, "Wouldn't it be wonderful if …" and then append the solution to your problem. Then spend some time in serious daydreaming, imagining what a world in which your dream had come true would be like. What would have happened? Who would have played a part? How would it have been achieved? How would it feel? Having developed this fantasy you then need to work on each of the obstacles which you can identify between you and your solution. We dealt with mapping obstacles earlier in the book.

 Obstacle mapping
see p. 31.

For some people the early training not to daydream has been so successful that they cannot move from problem solving mode into day dreaming. They find themselves developing arguments against all aspects of their fantasy. If this is happening when you try this technique, a good way around it is to switch on the right side of the brain and switch off the left. If there was a switch which could transfer dominance this would be an easy instruction to follow. Since there is no such switch we have a couple of suggestions to encourage the transfer.

Firstly, draw a picture of the solution to your problem. In someone who is good at drawing this will almost certainly involve switching off the left hand side of the brain. In someone who "cannot" draw there is a danger that the left hand side of the brain will be used for drawing. If you find yourself drawing representations of objects instead of what you actually see then this is probably the case. A solution to this is to read Betty Edwards' excellent book. She has a number of techniques for switching to the right hand side. Another approach is to use our second suggestion below.

 Drawing a problem?
Try Betty Edwards, *Drawing on the Right Side of your Brain* (Collins, 1986).

Try coping with your internal censor by making a collage of the solution to your problem. Forget about the problem in hand. Go through a range of illustrated magazines, catalogues and other sources of pictures and find any appealing image. Don't worry about why it appeals, just cut it out. Having got a pile of appealing images, start sticking them together into a collage which describes a solution to your problem. This feels a lot like playing around but it is an extremely effective way of overcoming our natural tendency to evaluate too soon. This approach also works well with groups who find that working alongside others who are playing the same game inspires them to develop more fantastic solutions.

We have found that this technique on its own does not generally solve problems. It does do two things, though. Firstly it provides a source of energy for developing a solution. There is nothing as mobilizing for an individual or group as a dream. A dream of their problem solved can sometimes be the spur needed to work towards a solution. The second thing this technique does is to provide a source of novel, even absurd, directions in which to look for a solution. If the solutions you have been generating are prosaic, then fantasy is a good way of broadening your scope.

TIMEOUT

Failure – Oersted

Hans Christian Oersted failed to demonstrate the independence of electricity and magnetism in a public lecture in 1819. Since this is what he was setting out to do this could have been an embarrassing failure. Instead of covering up the error and moving on, he postulated that the world might be wrong in believing the two things to be independent.

A different view

Take a stiff problem you are facing, find a friend or colleague who knows nothing about it and ask them for advice. Ignorance can be a powerful aid. It can be particularly illuminating to ask a child.

Someone else's problem

This is another bridging technique which involves changing your perspective. In this case, you take on the persona of someone who is completely detached from your problem; preferably someone who not only does not understand the problem but does not understand the world in which the problem exists. This means that they are more likely to ask stupid questions about your reasons for doing things.

Start by selecting a character who is unconnected with your problem. Spend a little time getting into the role of the character. Know what they would know. Think what they would think. Be them for a while. Having done this, return to your problem. You will have to explain the basis of the problem and the world in which the problem exists to this character, but do not bother with too much detail. It is important that they remain somewhat detached. A quick aerial survey will cover the salient points. Having done all of this, get them to start suggesting what solutions to the problem might look like in their world. Use these solutions to move towards something which will work in yours.

The next question is, how do you pick a character? To be honest anyone who is detached from your problem will do. If you know a lot about them that is useful but not essential. To start you off we have provided a list of 60 characters here. The advantage of lists which are 60 long is that you can use the second hand of your watch to select an item. Wherever it is pointing right now, take that number and use the corresponding item in the list – but do choose your own too.

Aerial survey

See p. 35.

Mayflower view

Try asking one of the Pilgrim Fathers for new ways of selling soap.

60 seconds

The 60 second selector is widely used by Edward de Bono and other creativity gurus.

 1 Mae West
 2 Queen Elizabeth the First
 3 A prostitute in Paris
 4 Adolf Hitler
 5 Attila the Hun
 6 A librarian
 7 William Shakespeare
 8 Macbeth
 9 A Roman centurion
10 A plumber
11 Dr Livingstone
12 Marilyn Monroe
13 Forrest Gump
14 The President of the United States
15 A pet rabbit
16 A mass murderer
17 A prison warder
18 John Wayne
19 The Lone Ranger
20 Robin Hood
21 A computer programmer
22 Snoopy
23 Ludwig van Beethoven
24 Karl Marx
25 Groucho Marx
26 Niccolo Machiavelli
27 Albert Schweitzer
28 George Washington
29 A nasturtium
30 A surgeon
31 The head teacher of a large inner city school
32 A circus clown
33 A circus trapeze artist
34 A poet
35 A Roman Catholic priest
36 A Rabbi
37 Confucius
38 Frank Lloyd Wright
39 Sherlock Holmes
40 Hercule Poirot
41 A martian
42 Winston Churchill
43 Count Dracula
44 Mao Tse Tung
45 Billy the Kid
46 Tutankhamen
47 Charles Darwin
48 An ant
49 A court jester
50 Orville Wright
51 Paul McCartney
52 Neil Armstrong
53 A blind person
54 A deaf person
55 Lucille Ball
56 Donald Duck
57 A New York cab driver
58 The Pope
59 Superman
60 A beggar in Bombay

 **TIMEOUT**

Instant pictures

Edwin Land was on holiday with his family when his young daughter demanded to see the photographs he was taking. She could not understand why she was not allowed to see them straight away. Land immediately hit on the idea of an instant camera. Making it practical took a little longer.

This story is often told as an example of inspiration out of the blue. I prefer to think of it as showing the power of the gestation of ideas. Land had been working with a light polarizer he called Polaroid, since 1926 when he was a freshman at Harvard. He formed the Polaroid Corporation in 1937 but the Polaroid camera did not appear until 1947.

It's just like ...

The final bridging technique is to use analogy and metaphor to develop your thinking. To do this you associate your problem strongly with another event or object. You then work on solving your problem as if it really were that event or object. It is important that you do not pick an event or object because you have already seen a similarity. You must pick something where you have to work to force a fit.

As an example, assume that you have said that your problem is just like a game of football. Work on force fitting similarities between a football game and the problem. Who are the players opposing one another? Who are the supporters cheering them on? What is the hapless ball being kicked from one end to another? What is a goal? Who or what is the referee? Who trains, coaches, manages and pays for the performance?

Find any and every similarity you can and then ask yourself what you would do in the world of football to move towards a solution to this problem. Do not try for rationality yet. Remember this is essentially an irrational process. Just let fly with all of the solutions that the analogy presents. Once you have collected the volume of ideas you can start to work them towards feasibility.

Again, we have provided you with a list of 60 analogies. There is absolutely nothing special about these. Any analogies which allow a strong mental image will work fine. Try flicking through a dictionary as an alternative.

Bridge:
- Fantasy
- Someone else's problem
- It's just like …

1 A telephone
2 A matchbox
3 A chair
4 A computer
5 A Ferris wheel
6 A television set
7 A chocolate teapot
8 A briefcase
9 A wheel
10 A pocket calculator
11 A graveyard
12 A pot plant
13 A grand piano
14 A sweet shop
15 A deck chair
16 A splinter in your finger
17 A roaring log fire
18 A snow drift
19 A dull party
20 A street lamp
21 An oasis in the desert

22 A street map
23 A calendar
24 A firing squad
25 A condemned man's last meal
26 A clockwork train set
27 A wild cat
28 A faulty parachute
29 A dustbin
30 A bathroom mirror
31 An electric socket
32 A hammer
33 A burst balloon
34 A credit card
35 An ill-fitting shoe
36 A kitchen table
37 A garden gate
38 The smoke from a bonfire
39 A carpet
40 A Christmas tree
41 A fountain pen

42 A computer instruction manual
43 A wilted rose
44 A beehive
45 A country stream
46 A suspension bridge
47 An alarm clock
48 A bar of soap
49 A moth by a candle flame
50 A long cold drink
51 The film in a camera
52 The iris of your eye
53 A pile of elephant dung
54 A clock which runs slow
55 A filing cabinet
56 A cuddly toy
57 An artist's palette
58 The human brain
59 A banana skin
60 A snail's shell

Privet hedge beds

A designer of beds wanted to achieve a particular springing effect and found the answer in a privet hedge. The pattern of twigs and leaves achieved the effect the designer was looking for and could be directly transferred to the plastic materials suitable for bedding.

TIMEOUT

By-pass

- *Random word*
- *Random picture*
- *Found objects*
- *Nonsense sentence*

By-pass
The by-pass has come
to embody the impact
of the impersonal
planner on real life:
hence the hyperspace
by-pass in Douglas
Adams, *Hitchhiker's
Guide to the Galaxy*
(Pan Books, 1979).

The by-pass techniques are similar to the bridging techniques but they do not involve story telling, characterization or analogy in the same way. The similarity is that they do involve kicking you aside from the course you had planned by forcing a by-pass around obstacles. There is, as with the last two bridging techniques, a certain amount of random stimulation involved. In the case of the bridging techniques you could choose to pick at random or deliberately. In the case of the by-pass techniques random selection is important to success.

There are four techniques in this section: random word, random picture, found objects and nonsense sentence.

Random word

This is one of the most commonly used creativity techniques. Its popularity stems from two sources: firstly it is very easy to use; and secondly it is very effective. The danger is that it can become the mainstay of your creative thinking and always using the same method for generating creative thoughts is likely to lead to staleness. For that reason our advice for this technique is to use it but not to fall in love with it. Remember all of the other tools in your toolkit and make effective use of them.

**Random
stimulation**
Figures heavily in
creativity techniques.
Any method that you
can use to kick yourself
out of your current
patterns of thought
could be useful. A
random stimulation
almost guarantees a
significant step.

The random word technique involves selecting a word at random (surprised?) and using that as the stimulus for moving thinking away from your problem. Having selected the word, you list all of the associations and ideas which spring to mind as a result of the word. There need not be any sensible link. Having said this, there was at least one occasion where we had to stop a creative idea generating session to ask why a link had been given. It was just too intriguing. Our word was "elephant" and one woman in the group had given the link of "naked man." You can understand how hard it was just to write this up and move on. So we asked why. She replied, "What did the elephant say to the naked man? – Cute, but it'll never pick up peanuts!" You see, any link, however bizarre, will do.

TIMEOUT

Misunderstanding – balloons

In 1783 the Montgolfier brothers demonstrated their hot air balloon to Marie Antoinette and King Louis XVI. The King wanted a balloon of his own so ordered his scientific officer, Monsieur Jacques Alexandre César Charles, to develop one. Charles had not seen the Montgolfier balloon and the King was unable to describe the scientific principles which allowed it to fly so his work had to start from scratch. In the process he used the newly discovered gas, hydrogen, since this was lighter than air, and invented the hydrogen balloon.

Having generated a whole list of links to the random word and ideas around the random word, try to relate them back to the problem. Allow any and every idea which springs to mind as a result of them to generate ideas. In the case of the naked man, how would taking your clothes off help or hinder developing a solution? Force-fit linkages and later they can be developed into solutions.

Yet again, the question arises, how do you develop a random word? We have provided another list of 60 items. Remember, though, that there are many other ways of working this. We find that nouns work better than other words and that the broader and more emotional the link, the better. The method of selection is for your preference. One consultant we know takes a dictionary with him to creative problem solving sessions and makes a theatrical performance of selecting the word. His thinking is that it makes it absolutely clear that there is no association between the word and the problem. You will find, though, that usually when you use this technique you will think afterwards that you were lucky to have picked the word you did because it generated so many ideas. The technique just works that way.

Random word
Take the word "bullet." Jot down some associations. Now consider the problem of keeping staff happy in a time of change. What sort of ideas do the bullet associations spark?

Random words
The sheer randomness of these techniques misses whole swathes of possibilities. To start with this can be unsettling. It's important to remember that there is unlikely to be a single right answer. If you develop a great idea, does it really matter that you've missed half a dozen others?

1 Soap	13 Jazz	25 Cigarette	37 Knife
2 Mouse	14 Hat	26 Toy	38 Smoke
3 Cloud	15 Credit card	27 Snow	39 President
4 Hair	16 Church	28 Parachute	40 Button
5 Ice cream	17 Shop	29 Door	41 Eagle
6 Rocket	18 Hamburger	30 Tap	42 Taxi
7 Tax	19 Book	31 Hurricane	43 Soup
8 Bed	20 Scales	32 Watch	44 Prison
9 Wheel	21 Coal	33 Balloon	45 Shark
10 Frog	22 Camel	34 Party	46 Diamond
11 Farm	23 Diary	35 Shoe	47 Gun
12 Computer	24 Lawyer	36 Root	48 Train

"One picture is worth more than a thousand words." (Chinese proverb)

Random picture

Take a color magazine and flick to the first page after p. 23 which contains a sizable photograph. Look at it, overall and in detail. Now jot down some associations. Use these to spark ideas on ways of increasing production in a bakery.

Back to school

Can't be bothered to put together a picture portfolio? Give the task to your children or a friend's children as a holiday project.

TIMEOUT

Lone objects

If using this technique alone, find three objects.

49 Picture	52 Nose	55 Rose	58 Camera
50 Beer	53 Elephant	56 Saw	59 Banana
51 Kitchen	54 Wine	57 Hospital	60 Snail

Random picture

The next random stimulation is pictorial. The random picture technique involves choosing an image at random, then generating links from this which will be used to produce solutions.

This technique works in exactly the same fashion as random word. Selecting an image is harder than selecting a word but it can prove worth the effort. A picture is open to broader interpretation than a word, unclear or evocative pictures even more so. If we take the Chinese proverb to be true, then we've a thousand words, each to act as springboards to inspiration.

We cannot provide you with 60 pictures without pushing up the cost of this book by a significant amount. The solution is for you to find them yourself. Go through magazines, catalogues and your photo albums and take out as many pictures as you can that evoke a range of images (as opposed to personal memories) for you. They need not be appealing pictures, disturbing ones work just as effectively. Alternatively, buy a photography book from a remaindered bookshop to get an instant portfolio of pictures.

Misunderstanding – telephones

In 1876 Alexander Graham Bell was awarded the patent for the telephone. When he started his work he thought that he was merely reproducing what had been done earlier by the German physicist Johann Reis. It was only when he was a long way down the path of developing the instrument that he discovered he had misunderstood the German paper he had read and that Reis could transmit musical notes but not the human voice.

Found objects

This by-pass technique uses the world around you as a random stimulation. You could use it on your own, although we've never tried it that way, but it is ideally suited to groups. The group is sent out with the instruction to each come back with an object which they can talk about. The object can be anything that they can find. These objects are used as a stimulation for generating ideas.

The generation of ideas using this technique deserves a little explanation. We have used found objects as quick fire link generators in the way that random words and random pictures are used, but find that they are most effective if the person who has brought the object back has a chance to explain what significance it has and why they brought it, and describes at least one idea which it generates for them. This gives a foundation on which others can build their ideas. It is also probably best if everyone has the chance to present their object before the group moves on to building on selected ideas and quick fire link generation. This is because everyone will have at least half of their mind on how they are going to present their own object to the group. Until this is done you will not have their full attention.

Once you have generated links and some initial ideas you can develop the links into ideas in the same way as we did with the previous techniques. We will develop ideas further in the waymarking section.

Nonsense sentence

This is a technique which only exists in this book because of some work we were doing on using computers to help with idea generation. We have developed a series of small computer programs that help to generate ideas, one of which deals with nonsense sentences. You do not need a computer to make use of this technique, however.

The program we wrote generates sentences which are either wholly or partially nonsensical. These sentences are then used as a springboard to allow you to move away from a problem into other areas. We have provided 60 examples of such sentences, generated by the program, at the end of this section.

None of these mean anything or are meant to mean anything and they were merely the output of the first 60 sentences generated by the program. The notion is that, because of the amazing ability of the mind to see patterns even where none exist, we can force such nonsense sentences to make sense. Take any one of the sentences and describe it to yourself. Tell yourself that it is real. Develop a complete

Energy provider

It is interesting how the found objects technique generates a high level of energy in a group. In part it is because they are getting up and doing something – not just sitting around. Also, it seems to be that people genuinely enjoy playing show and tell.

Nonsense at work

Use this technique with the phrase "A sharp fectol." See how the nature of this imaginary thing might help with ideas for selecting which of three office sites is to be closed down to save your firm money.

description of the object. Now use that object as a direct means of solving the problem, or to generate links in the same way as you used in the random word technique. At first it is hard to convince yourself that the sentence is anything but nonsense. Do give it a try. Push yourself. You will be surprised at the links your mind makes.

If you want to use this technique, you can use our list or you can generate nonsense sentences using only the power of your imagination. Alternatively, you can do what the program does. Develop a list of acceptable phonemes to start words, form the middle of words and end words. Develop a list of partial sentences, then, at random, create words and stubs of sentences and join them into a nonsense whole. The exercise can be instructive in itself. It is interesting to see which combinations sound like real sentences and which are one level of abstraction too far from reality.

1 A wobbly cooth
2 A floating hiawd
3 A klailly telephone
4 A strousmly typewriter for use in cooking
5 A potted ciapre
6 A criecrly booklet
7 The remains of a gargantuan graegy bought with a credit card
8 The first ever bronze smoudy belonging to a child
9 A miabling double decker bus
10 A spooglly kairp
11 A treernly waste bin for use by the army
12 A weechly rubber plant
13 A spaigly onion
14 A skrurtly banana
15 A poor man's theed
16 A vountly pig
17 A liahly toothbrush with a broken top
18 A potted furb to replace a standard parachute
19 A phoobraing pair of spectacles
20 A scrourcly abacus which is cracked
21 A cleephly staple gun
22 A mouyly kitchen appliance belonging to a child
23 A caged saeple for use on the beach
24 A soching strunk
25 A seehly picture frame
26 An escaped rair

27 A long wouh
28 A blue bliev displayed on a postage stamp
29 An Australian taegh
30 A shiny golden troof
31 A long phoop for use as camouflage
32 A sklewly wut
33 A knielly dental hygiene assistant for attaching to a bike
34 A tourlly smoov
35 A zoozly pair of spectacles left unused and unloved
36 A gilded scriam to keep in sheep
37 A plouwding lioness
38 A gheiscrly spanner
39 A voofly carpet for slowing a speeding car
40 A wiaping flurve
41 The only absolutely square schoorm
42 A zeeyly steeg
43 A kneechly desk which solves quadratic equations
44 A fnoorvly typewriter
45 A fnaeschly car
46 The remains of a gargantuan crarf
47 A baid with which to stroorze a zaerp
48 A sleirming calendar
49 A scantily clad shoch which has been sandpapered smooth
50 A plirdly spanner
51 A giebraly toothbrush
52 An intricately woven frurd for quieting your noisy neighbors
53 A scheinly spanner with no top
54 A hosly thraig
55 A gniaghly pair of spectacles
56 A wraking scrible
57 A remote controlled quak which is cracked
58 A smelly wrekle for use as camouflage
59 A fast scliri
60 An African tribal tharv for tangle free hair

By pass:
- Random word
- Random picture
- Found objects
- Nonsense sentence.

Creativity blockers – tunnel vision

 **TIMEOUT**

It's easy to think of uncreative thought as a miner crawling through a cramped tunnel with the "nugget," the solution, just above his head through the rock. This is a bad analogy. It would be far better to think of a broad and well trodden tunnel with thousands of pedestrians marching through it. The nugget they are searching for may be off to one side or may be above their heads but the issue is that they are unlikely to search for it there with an army of their fellows marching forward.

The creative solution is not where you would expect to find it. If it were, someone else would have found it already. Being focussed and looking for the solution in conventional ways will only reinforce the well trodden path. As de Bono points out, you need a provocation of some sort to help you break out of this well trodden path. Once away from the path it is easier to scout around until you find the nugget. Having found it, building a new tunnel back onto the track is not difficult. This is the reason why creative ideas seem obvious in hindsight. It is galling the number of times you can work really hard to come up with a truly new and novel solution which is so obvious after the event that the reaction to it is, "So what?" Still, at least you know that the solution would not have been found without you.

■ New destination

- *Fantasy destination*
- *Another destination*

So far we have covered tunneling techniques, bridging techniques and by-pass techniques. We now move on to look at finding a new destination. Within this last part of building there are two distinct types of new destination. The first is a fantasy destination which is used in the way that other techniques in this chapter have been used, to stimulate ideas. The other is to consider another destination, a technique which aims more at questioning the problem you are trying to solve.

Fantasy destination

This is a fun technique. It is far too enjoyable to count as real work. It is most effective with a group, but will work when you are on your own as long as you can play around with the idea enough. To use it well takes a significant amount of time, at least two hours, but it is very effective at generating novel solutions. Given the time it takes it is best to be sure that you really do want novel solutions before embarking on this path.

> **New destinations**
>
> It's a sobering thought that the world is increasingly short of new destinations. Perhaps that's why we particularly like science fiction/fantasy as a means of stimulating original ideas. Tom Peters has suggested that it would be well worth hiring in a science fiction author to help a company with new ideas.

The way that the technique works is that you redefine the problem you are facing as being similar to a fantasy problem which does not or could not happen in the real world. Getting major departments to line up behind a corporate vision could be seen as teaching hippos to dance to the Nutcracker Suite. Improving telephone answering times could be seen as getting planets to revolve around the sun faster than they currently do. Increasing your savings could be seen as inventing a machine which could steal gold fillings without the victim ever noticing.

There are two points about the fantasy destination. It must have some, extremely tenuous, link to your problem as stated. And it must be obviously absurd – the more absurd, the better.

Having stated the problem you must now find solutions. You have the full armory of the techniques listed above at your disposal. The only real advice here is that you should strive for solutions which are even sillier than the fantasy destination. The more fun you have with this technique the more effective it will be.

At the end of a session trying to solve your fantastic problem you will have recorded a large number of very silly solutions. The trick now is to continue the enjoyment and to have a lighthearted approach to turning these solutions into ways of approaching or solving your real problem. The link need not be cast iron, it could be a fairly tenuous one. It might be that there is no obvious link but you or one of your group has made a creative leap and been inspired by one of the fantasy solutions. At this point, take whatever presents itself. Do not evaluate where the idea comes from or how the link is made.

Typically you will finish this process with some ideas which can be used as they stand and a whole collection of ideas which are wonderfully appealing but not at all feasible. There are techniques listed in the waymarking section which might be of use in developing these. The key message is do not reject appealing but impossible ideas because they are often the source of truly novel solutions.

Another destination

At school we are taught that there is one right answer to a problem. We also learn that the teacher already knows this answer and that our

Self-expression vs structure
There is no right answer here. Allowing full self-expression is no way to teach anything, yet being prescriptive inevitably closes down creativity. Arguably the best approach is to continue to teach "the right answer" but also teach creativity as a discipline.

job is to find the same one as he or she has in mind. Most people can remember an occasion at school when they had a right answer to a question but because it was not the one in the mind of the teacher it became "wrong."

Another destination is a technique for moving us away from this mind set and asking what is another right answer – or, in this case, what is another right question. We have spent time expressing our problem using the surveying tools. We have a problem statement or series of problem statements which we are working at finding solutions to. This technique says, "What if that isn't our problem? What if our problem is really somewhere else entirely?"

In asking the question it is usually enough then to merely search for other problems which might be causing the difficulties we are experiencing. You might want to use some of the other techniques listed above, particularly the by-pass techniques, to help you to find other sources of your problem. Naturally, the reason for trying to find other sources for the problem is that these then become a new destination, enabling us to avoid the obstacles which were in the way before (though possibly generating a whole new batch).

New destination:

- Fantasy destination
- Another destination.

PUTTING THE TOOLKIT INTO PRACTICE

Throughout our descriptions of the various techniques we have tried to suggest ways to use them on your own or working with groups. Now we'll give a short overview, encompassing all of the techniques, which will look at the approach to building and how that might differ from case to case.

Before you use any of the techniques you must allow time to list out any ideas for solutions which you already have. It would be silly to think that in addressing a problem the only possible solutions are generated by off-the-wall techniques. One of the people you are working with may already have an ideal solution just waiting to be picked up.

If you are going to work with a group on solving problems, the first piece of advice is to do more than read this chapter. We are laying out techniques for solving problems and for generating ideas but there is far more to facilitating a group than this. There are some

10 minutes
Just want a quick idea? If it's a new product to add to your line, try the level chain in surveying. Otherwise pick a building technique at random and spend five minutes applying it, five minutes sifting the ideas. Don't always use the same technique – they'll become stale.

excellent books on developing facilitation skills and we would strongly recommend that you read one of these. Before doing that, take a look at the chapter on group creativity.

Group creativity
See p. 163.

The next piece of advice is, as with any skill, practice in a safe environment. If you can start with a relatively easy problem and with friends in the group, you can see for yourself what works and what doesn't before it becomes too big an issue. Try out a range of techniques and a variety of ways of handling them. The more exposure you can get before you tackle the really big issues with an important group, the better it will be.

The last piece of advice about dealing with groups is that you look after yourself. If you are facilitating a group in solving a problem there is a tendency to feel solely responsible for the outputs of the group. You are not. The group is responsible and your role as facilitator is merely to channel their energy, through appropriate processes and techniques, into developing a solution. As long as you have done this in the best way possible then you have done all that could be asked of you. Do not berate yourself for the things the group did or did not do. They are big boys and girls and they made the choices they made. If you do not reach a solution it is more down to them than to you.

If you are working alone on solving a problem or generating ideas, it is worth envisaging facilitating a meeting with yourself. You need to be as aware of the process being used when you are alone, as when you are in a group. It's easy for the content to overwhelm you, pushing out the process. We have heard problem content described as being like honey: it is sweet and attractive but it is also very sticky. It is an awful job to get clean of the stuff once you've plunged your hand in. Keep half of your mind on the problem solving or idea generation process while the other half dives into the content. This is tricky but nothing that a fully fledged creative individual like you can't handle.

TIMEOUT

Nature

According to Gordon Edge of PA Technology, "If you want to solve a problem, see how it is solved in nature. Living forms always have the most economical answers as a result of evolution."

His team has used the way in which a nocturnal moth's eye absorbs light and does not reflect it, by means of a delicate criss-cross pattern coating the eye, as the basis for an information storage system on an optical disk.

Key words

Tunnel: challenge assumption; distortion; reversal.

Bridge: fantasy; someone else; just like.

By-pass: random word/picture/object; nonsense.

New destination: fantasy, second.

Coming soon ➤ ➤ ➤

In the waymarking section which follows we will take the ideas that have been generated during building and refine them, highlighting good points and ironing out flaws.

FROM NORTHANGER ABBEY

By Jane Austen

The progress of the friendship between Catherine and Isabella was quick as its beginning had been warm, and they passed so rapidly through every gradation of increasing tenderness, that there was shortly no fresh proof of it to be given to their friends or themselves. They called each other by their Christian name, were always arm in arm when they walked, pinned up each other's train for the dance, and were not to be divided in the set; and if a rainy morning deprived them of other enjoyments, they were still resolute in meeting in defiance of wet and dirt, and shut themselves up, to read novels together. Yes, novels; – for I will not adopt that ungenerous and impolitic custom so common with novel writers, of degrading by their contemptuous censure the very performances, to the number of which they are themselves adding – joining with their greatest enemies in bestowing the harshest epithets on such works, and scarcely ever permitting them to be read by their own heroine, who, if she accidentally take up a novel, is sure to turn over its insipid pages with disgust. Alas! if the heroine of one novel be not patronized by the heroine of another, from whom can she expect protection and regard? I cannot approve of it. Let us leave it to the Reviewers to abuse such effusions of fancy at their leisure, and over every new novel to talk in threadbare strains of the trash with which the press now groans. Let us not desert one another; we are an injured body.

Although our productions have afforded more extensive and unaffected pleasure than those of any other literary corporation in the world, no species of composition has been so much decried. From pride, ignorance, or fashion, our foes are almost as many as our readers. And while the abilities of the nine-hundredth abridger of the History of England, or of the man who collects and publishes in a volume some dozen lines of Milton, Pope, and Prior, with a paper from the Spectator and a chapter from Sterne, are eulogized by a thousand pens, there seems almost a general wish of decrying the capacity and undervaluing the labour of the novelist, and of slighting the performances which have only genius, wit and taste to recommend them. "I am no novel reader – I seldom look into novels – Do not imagine that *I* often read novels – It is really very well for a novel" – Such is the common cant. "And what are you reading, Miss"? "Oh! it is only a novel!" replies the young lady; while she lays down her book with affected indifference, or momentary shame. "It is only Cecilia, or Camilla, or Belinda;" or, in short, only some work in which the greatest powers of the mind are displayed, in which the most thorough knowledge of human nature, the happiest delineation of its varieties, the liveliest effusions of wit and humor

 TALE PIECE

 Early humor

Jane Austen is often remembered as a writer of costume romances, ignoring the strong element of humor which, once the style of the period is penetrated, is often funnier than the efforts of Victorian writers, despite their relative closeness in time.

The practice of stepping back from the fiction and making asides to the reader is common in modern humor.

 More early modernism

Another device Austen uses is to refer forward to an incident, a technique used heavily by Douglas Adams. For example:

"He cannot be the instigator of the three villains in horsemen's great coats, by whom she will hereafter be forced into a travelling-chaise and four, which will drive off with incredible speed." (Jane Austen, *Northanger Abbey*)

Key thoughts

- Take a step above the action into the meta-world which creates it
- There's often a gap between people's statements and beliefs
- Balance process and content.

are conveyed to the world in the best chosen language. Now, had the same young lady been engaged with a volume of the Spectator, instead of such a work, how proudly would she have produced the book, and told its name; though the chances must be against her being occupied by any of that voluminous publication, of which either the matter or manner would not disgust a young person of taste: the substance of its papers so often consisting in the statement of improbable circumstances, unnatural characters, and topics of conversation, which no longer concern anyone living; and their language, too, frequently so coarse as to give no very favorable idea of the age that could endure it.

WAYMARKING

■ **Signs along the way**

■ **Waymarking toolkit**

■ **How to put it together**

Sirens

In Greek mythology the sirens were half-bird, half-woman creatures who lured sailors onto the rocks with their sweet singing. It is fairly unlikely that they had a song called *Expediency*.

SIGNS ALONG THE WAY

Creativity is a dangerous companion. It sings the siren song of expediency. Fired by new ideas from the building stage, it is easy to rush into action. The simple fact that you have decided to take a creative approach suggests that you are more inclined to action than analysis. But just as the investment of time in preparing the surveying proved worthwhile, so will the opportunity to take a brief step back from idea generation before rushing into activity.

In Imagination Engineering terms, we are ready to mark the way with signs and facilities, transforming the path from a crude track to a fully functional, navigable route. The function of this activity is twofold. In the first place it's an opportunity to take a breather after the frantic pace of creation and assess what has been produced. Secondly, the waymarking stage allows for some fine-tuning, ensuring that the best possible solution has been arrived at.

WAYMARKING TOOLKIT

■ Summary

Stagecoach signs

A few of these still exist, looking odd to modern eyes as the need to be read from the top of a coach means that they are placed high in the air.

Stakeholders

An independent party with whom each of those who makes a wager deposits the money etc. wagered (*Concise Oxford Dictionary*, OUP).

The tools for waymarking are less technical than those of the surveying and building stages. This has a good parallel in the real world. The technologies to survey a route and to construct the road or rail track have changed immensely, and continue to advance. In comparison, marking the way sometimes seems hardly to have moved on from the pointers that guided stagecoaches from town to town.

This can, of course, be a false impression. Visibility and reflectivity have been transformed to meet the needs of modern traffic, but the analogy holds good, because the essence of waymarking is the written word, communication between people, and as such is more about thoughts and ideas than precision measurements and accurate cutting.

The Imagination Engineering tools which contribute to waymarking are fivefold:

- **The slip road** – there's no point having a host of solutions you can't get started on. If you have generated a large range of ideas, the slip road leads you to the right starting point.

- **The washroom** – getting a gut feel for your proposed approach.
- **Viewpoints** – looking outwards: going beyond your own views to those of the other stakeholders in the enterprise.
- **Signposts** – highlighting everything that's good about the proposal.
- **Hazard markers** – looking for the potential stumbling blocks and problems which may make your idea impractical.

■ The slip road

At the end of the building stage you are left with a set of ideas. The first part of waymarking involves selecting the ideas that you want to move forward with and make workable.

Which ideas you select depends on your objectives. If you are looking for novel solutions, focus on those ideas that are appealing, giving no thought as to how workable they are. If any answer will do, focus on those ideas that are most workable. Bear in mind, though, that it is much easier to make an appealing idea workable than it is to make a workable idea appealing.

Creativity blockers – you

The reasoning behind many of the techniques listed here is that one of the biggest obstacles to your creativity is what you know. You already know what will work and what will not, so you ignore the avenues which explore the impossible or improbable. This is an essential mental characteristic for dealing with everyday life. If you did not do this you would spend your whole time starting from first principles and would never get out of bed in the morning.

A caveman walks into an unknown cave and is mauled by the lion that lives there, barely escaping with his life. He tells the rest of his tribe and from then on the whole tribe are more wary about how they enter caves. They have learned that caves may provide shelter and safety but they are potentially dangerous. Imagine again that the caveman and the tribe do not learn. Imagine that they are truly creative every moment of their

 Slip road exercise

Using one of the building techniques, generate as many ideas as you can in five minutes for the problem "devise a new way of selling food." Then set up three or four slip roads, first on preference, then on practicality.

 TIMEOUT

"Habit is either the best of servants or the worst of masters." (Nathaniel Emmons)

 Dealing with life

See the tale piece, "The Death of Sleep" on p. 89.

waking lives: there would be no cavemen and some very fat cave lions. This is not only true of the dangerous world of the caveman, you too face situations every day which if you experimented would lead to you dying swiftly. Learning from experience is essential, you need to do it in order to survive. The drawback in learning from experience is that we often generalize our learning to relate it to situations where it does not apply. Worse still, the world changes and our past experience ceases to be valid. Whatever the reason, learning from experience can inhibit creativity. If it were not necessary for survival we might try to dispense with it altogether. In order to create you must be able to develop beyond what you know, making a new knowledge base. You need to know what could be, or even what could not be (but just might), rather than what is.

Those techniques which start by denying reality work on this principle. They seem stupid. It is an obvious nonsense to explore the world by starting where the world is not: Trust us. These things work. You do come full circle back to a reality which is possible. The final destination is obvious with hindsight but often very different to where you might have been without using the technique.

If you decide to select by appeal, try a cash bidding method. Imagine you have £100 to spend on buying four or five of the ideas. Place the money on the ones which feel right. If you are tempted to spread your money too thinly, try a rule that you can't allocate the same amount to different options. This approach works particularly well if a group is involved in the waymarking process.

If you want a definitively workable answer, look at costs, benefits, and risk. Draw three columns alongside your ideas and for each quickly summarize these factors. How you weigh the choices will inevitably depend on your own attitude to risk, but using these factors you should be able to single out a small number of options for further consideration.

Whichever approach you take, it is important to reduce the number of ideas you take forward to no more than four or five. If necessary and if time allows you can always come back and select some more. Alternatively, if time is tight, you may whittle down the list to one or two. In either case, the slip road should be a very quick exercise, leading into the rest of waymarking.

■ The washroom

We toyed with a number of images to represent this concept in Imagination Engineering. The requirement is to step back from all the techniques and facts and use a very personal approach. In the washroom we are interested not in facts, but in feelings.

In translating this to the Imagination Engineering model, we wanted an aspect of finishing off the route that had nothing to do with the mode of transport, but was more about people. It could equally well have been a restaurant or pub, but there was something about the combination of a gut reaction and the washroom that provided a strong image.

This is the easiest task in the Imagination Engineering armory to perform, but it is very easy to overlook. What you need to do is take a step back, put away your papers, switch off your computer, ideally get a cup of coffee or a glass of your favorite drink and relax. Now think about your idea as a whole – what do you think of it? What's your immediate gut feel? You've heard of holistic medicine – this is holistic creativity. Don't analyse the solution in detail, just note down what you think and why it appeals.

It sounds so simple that it ought to be a piece of cake. Only it's not. Our analytical, show me the numbers, hard-nosed business approach doesn't fit well with this one. And yet feelings are a crucial part of any business decision.

Try it now. We're going to give you a handful of (very) outline business proposals. Don't think through the consequences, don't try to consider any of the contributing factors, just read through the proposal and decide "Do I like this idea? Does it work for me? Why do I like it (or not like it)?"

Proposal 1: A hotel franchise

A well-known, business hotel chain in an adjacent country wants to expand into your own. They are offering franchises, very reasonably priced for early adopters. They provide the fixtures and fittings and approach, you provide the site and management skills.

Proposal 2: Decision-making software

The head developer of a well-respected software company has pro-

 Relaxing
Many people find a bath at blood heat (around 37°C, 98.4°F) relaxing. Why not assess your ideas in the bath? Or take your team to a Jacuzzi.

 Getting away
The office is a terrible place for relaxed assessment. Take an idea you're currently working on out to the park or a restaurant for assessment.

 10 minutes
Not got time to get away from it all? Go and sit in your car, or the canteen or whatever place you can quickly find – away from your office but with comfortable chairs.

 The real thing
Two of these proposals are genuine, three fictional. Decide which are genuine. Does this influence your feelings?

totyped an impressive looking piece of decision-support software, which has no mass market equivalent. He would like to develop it into a commercial product and wants your financial backing.

Proposal 3: Biscandwiches

You are the CEO of a large food company. Your R and D department has come up with the concept of biscandwiches. These are pairs of biscuits (cookies) which the consumer can fill with their own fillings (supplied in separate pots).

Proposal 4: PC doctor service

A friend who is a personal computer expert is thinking of giving up his job and offering a service to homeworkers where (for a fee) he will help them out on the spot with PC problems. He has the technical knowledge, but what about the idea?

Proposal 5: Oil dispensers

Your multinational oil company is always trying to sell oil to customers, but they rarely buy it. You decide that this is because they have to buy a large can of oil, then take it to the car and put it in. To get round this you propose to fit your petrol pumps with oil dispensers which will provide measured amounts of oil just like the petrol pumps.

You might feel the washroom is unnecessary if you selected your ideas by preference in the first place, but it helps to be clear just why this particular approach tickles your fancy. Why is it the one for you?

■ Viewpoints

Very few exercises in creativity take place in total isolation. Even as apparently individual a creative act as writing a book or producing a painting will require the involvement of others – agents, publishers, galleries, critics – to succeed. Only if the creative output is to be hidden away in a cupboard and never seen will it be left to a single individual, and we would argue that this is not true creativity – that creativity requires a recipient as well as an originator.

On a real road, viewpoints are marked on the map – places where

Oil together
Some estimates suggest that the world's remaining oil reserves will only last 30–40 years at current consumption. Time for some creativity?

you can stop the car and get out to take a look at the scenery. Often they are situated in a high spot; always there should be beneficial views. In taking viewpoints, you will be looking at your ideas from the point of view of the others concerned.

First identify them. Write a short list of those involved: your boss, customers, co-workers – anyone who will be affected by the idea or have an input. If you get more than half a dozen on your list it's worth going through it again to trim down to the essentials. Too many viewpoints lead to confusion.

Now it's pretend time. Put yourself in their shoes. Imagine that you are them – or at the very least that you are an impersonator, trying to put across their essence on stage. Look at the idea from their viewpoint and get an idea of what they would think of it; how they might change it.

If this is a major project you will probably want to involve your stakeholders directly with questionnaires and interviews. If you are dealing with product design you may also like to observe the stake-holders interacting with product mock-ups in a usability lab. For a smaller undertaking it will be enough to imagine their response.

■ Signposts

Signposts point forwards; they lead you on in a positive fashion without worrying about where you've come from or how you are getting there. When using the signpost technique, you need to become totally optimistic, looking only for the good things in your proposal.

Many of us find this surprisingly difficult. It's all too easy to tear a concept apart; it's much harder to take it on board unquestioningly and find its benefits. This may be particularly true of European culture, which finds it easy to be self-critical.

When you signpost your idea, you need to put on a pair of rose-tinted spectacles, consciously and emphatically. If this is a group exercise, the facilitator will need to use considerable efforts to stop the negative creeping in. What's the point of this obsessive concentration on the positive? Identifying what's right with an idea enables us to build on its strengths, reinforcing the benefits. It's also particularly valuable before the final, hazard warning stage of waymarking,

 Viewpoints
Take the first activity in your next working day's schedule. Jot down a list of the stakeholders: if there are more than a handful, identify the key people.

 Usability labs
Fashionable in software design, the usability lab observes product users from unseen locations and notes their unprompted reactions. The lessons learned are often a shock to the designer.

 Good qualities
A highly successful management training program used by British Airways in the 1980s required attendees to say what was good about other members of their group. This exercise proved to have very strong bonding effects.

 Signposts
Think of a proposal which you have recently declined. Now signpost it – list its good points without any consideration of the bad. It can be a surprising exercise.

Hazard markers

Take the same proposal used in the signposting exercise. Assess the hazard markers, remembering to look for fixes, not just problems. Would you have treated the proposal any differently? Maybe not, but you have seen different sides of it.

which left to its own devices would shut down practically any new idea.

Just as you selected a handful of ideas, it is useful to focus on a handful of key signposts. Signs are great if sparsely provided, but a huge display of signs does more to confuse than assist.

■ Hazard markers

Every route has its hazards, specific sections of the journey which present unusual challenges, or even a whole direction which will provide problems for those navigating it. Hazard markers identify the problems ahead of time, warning us and making an appropriate response possible.

There's a similar need for hazard markers in Imagination Engineering. There will be flaws in your ideas. These may encompass a specific part of the approach, or may cover the entire idea. When setting up hazard markers you should first be flagging up the existence of problems, then offering solutions.

If the problems are minor it will be enough to note the required approach. For bigger hazards it may be necessary to revisit the building techniques, treating the hazard as a problem in its own right. In extreme cases, a hazard may be enough to shut down this particular idea. While it is very dangerous to shut down too soon – and this is why it's so important to identify the positives first in the signposting stage – there comes a point where you have to be prepared to drop an idea quickly. If the route is impassable don't linger, move on to one of the other selected ideas.

 **TIMEOUT**

Creativity blockers – school

What is your abiding memory of school? One of Paul's is the unfairness of a question which he got wrong in a test. "Our class was working on small, trial IQ tests in preparation for a major IQ test. One of the questions was to say which was the odd one out – a table, a chair, a stool, or a cat. Not surprisingly, my answer was a cat because the rest were inanimate pieces of furniture. The 'right' answer was a stool because it has three legs. I explained my thinking but I was still wrong. I was furious that the arbitrary decision of someone who was not bright enough to see the ambiguity in the question should mean that I was classified as having a lower IQ than I would otherwise have been."

That's how school is. In most cases there is a right answer to a question and the job of the class is to guess what is in the teacher's mind in order to be correct. In fairness, that is how it has to be. It would be impossible to manage a large class of children (or even a very small one) and allow full freedom to be totally creative. Think now of the training that this gives us and our children. There is a right answer and your job is to find it: once you have found it you have succeeded. In most cases in real life though there are many right answers. The best answer may be the second, third or fourth. School teaches us that these do not exist. Having found the right answer we stop and move on to the next problem.

The other overriding lesson we take from school is conformity. The good kids do what they are told and the bad kids do not. If you wish to do well at school you need to be a good kid. Bye-bye creativity.

 The real thing

Back in the washroom section we noted that two of the examples were genuine. If you need to know, it was proposals 1 and 2. However, since this book was first published, a food manufacturer has developed a biscandwich (with a more sensible name).

HOW TO PUT IT TOGETHER

First give yourself time for the waymarking stage. How much time will depend on the scale of the idea. Use a quick filter of the ideas generated in the previous stage to decide on your slip roads. Then take a comfort break in the washroom. What about the others involved – how will they feel? Look at the good points of your idea and the bad. How will you make things better?

You may by now have several concrete, clear ideas. This should not be looked on as a problem. Perhaps you need to get someone else's permission to go forward. If you are truly happy with all your ideas, leave it to them – give them a real choice for a change, instead of a list of options where only one is truly acceptable. If you need to choose yourself, revisit the washroom. One of your ideas may feel better than the rest. Take the opportunity to balance out the risks and opportunities to arrive at the best way forward.

If there is still nothing between them, ask someone else far removed from the problem, perhaps your spouse or children. Still not decided? Toss a coin. If the decision is this close, it's not worth agonising over.

Key words

Slip road; washroom;
viewpoints; signposts;
hazard markers; taking
a step back; creative
pause; refining.

Coming soon ➤➤➤

With your ideas tightened up and your tentative route transformed
into a clearly signed way, you are ready for the final stage of
Imagination Engineering – navigating. Give yourself a few minutes
for what you have read to sink in. Memory is a strange thing: check
out the tale piece.

TALE PIECE

THE DEATH OF SLEEP

By Paul Birch

I was born when I woke up this morning. I will die when I fall asleep this evening. That's not true of course, not in an objective sense. My body will survive, but the thing that is essentially me will have gone. I only know this because I have been told.

This morning I woke in a panic. I'm told that every morning I wake in a panic. I looked around at the dull green walls – two shades of green, presumably to break up the monotony. I realized I was in hospital: the green walls, the rows of beds and the medical paraphernalia were demonstration enough of that. My first thought was that I must have had an accident. The last memory I had was of speeding along a country lane on my Norton. I was going too fast, I had no helmet, but I knew that I was not going to lose control. Beyond that, try as hard as I might, I could remember nothing. OK, so I must have had an accident. It couldn't be too serious because I felt perfectly fit. I could feel no injuries, just a dull ache.

I looked down and saw an old man's hands and an old man's arms sticking out from under the bedclothes. They moved where my hands and arms should have moved, but they were not mine. I lifted my right hand. The old man's hand lifted in front of my face. I threw back the covers. The body in the bed was not mine, it belonged to an old man. That's when I panicked.

At the other end of the ward I vaguely heard a voice say, "He's awake. Go and calm him down." The voice was bored. This was a monotonous ritual for them.

Later it was explained to me that this same revelation has been happening on a daily basis for years. I had crashed my bike but that was over 30 years ago. I had suffered brain damage, affecting my memory. I can clearly remember my life before the accident. Not as *if* it was yesterday, it *was* yesterday as far as I am concerned. I can also remember what happens to me now but only for about 12 hours.

I started writing a short while ago. It's now afternoon. I have spent most of my day coming to terms with the fact that I lived a yesterday which no longer exists for me and that tomorrow I will remember nothing of this. This world is not entirely real. I am not me. I have been trapped inside the body of an old man in a world which I cannot understand. It is hard to believe that my slate will be wiped utterly clean.

It took the nurses a long time to convince me that I had lived 30 years of a life I could not remember. Thirty years on a day at a time basis, years that exist for everyone else but do not exist for me. They brought me an unfinished jigsaw puzzle which they tell me I started yesterday. I slowly packed it

Memory

Have you ever considered how much of your personality and the essential you is dependent upon what you can remember? You could not live a normal life without memory. What do you have to remember? What could you usefully forget?

Neurological damage

For a very personal and moving view of the effects of all sorts of neurological damage see Oliver Sacks, *The Man Who Mistook His Wife For a Hat* (Pan Books, 1986).

Key thoughts

- Experience and creativity are complementary
- Knowledge can limit your effective creativity.

back into its box. Where's the fun in finishing a puzzle that someone else started?

I am writing this in a journal which I am told is mine. I wanted to provide myself with some continuity when I wake tomorrow. Looking back through the journal I can see that I have written an almost identical note hundreds of times before. For a while the weight of depression and self-pity make me contemplate suicide. But what's the point? All I need to do is fall asleep.

NAVIGATING

- **Getting there**

- **Navigating toolkit**

- **How to put it together**

GETTING THERE

Creative

Showing imagination as well as routine skill. (*Concise Oxford Dictionary*, OUP).

What about art?

If you accept that art is a form of communication, then it too cannot be creative without being delivered (and appreciated).

In the previous chapter we pointed out a danger that accompanies creativity. It's easy to get an idea and rush in. But it's equally easy to generate a whole heap of ideas – or a single excellent one – and do nothing about it. We'd like to challenge the dictionary definition of being creative and say that it isn't enough to be imaginative, there simply isn't any creativity without implementation.

This makes the title of this book ring a little hollow, because what we're saying is that being imaginative doesn't make you creative in itself. We'll let you into a secret – the original title was Creativity Unleashed, but Imagination Engineering sounded better. That's a bit of waymarking in action. Whatever the book is called, the message is the same – no implementation, no creativity.

But surely this can't be right? Can't a creative person enjoy creativity for the pure idea? Only if there's a mental implementation under way, and that's hardly likely to be enough in any business application.

For the final stage of Imagination Engineering we consider the route to have been constructed. Now we intend to travel along it. We have used the term navigating to span the whole range of possibilities for travel. It's quite common, thanks to the use of the term "navigator" meaning one who keeps you on course, to forget that navigating is the action of travelling itself. Admittedly in its original form this was limited to the sea, but we're taking a broader approach.

NAVIGATING TOOLKIT

■ Summary

The navigating toolkit enables you to plan and execute your journey. Although there will be different approaches required for different journey types, the principal steps will always be the same. Decide what you are going to do (this is different from coming up with an idea; now we are considering the actions you will need to take, not the idea which inspired those actions). Then do it, noting how you are getting on.

Traditionally for larger undertakings this process has been very mechanistic. We will look at this approach – we've called it the check box method – but we will present an alternative which is growing in popularity all the time. There's nothing wrong with the check box approach, in fact for some long-term requirements it is the only practical way to move forward, but it lacks flexibility and as such does not react particularly well to volatile implementation areas, or to a problem where we have limited information and so cannot plan in any great detail.

Check boxes
The boxes in a list which you check (tick in the UK) when a task is completed.

Leonardo da Vinci

Leonardo da Vinci's technique for generating ideas was to shut his eyes, relax and scribble on a piece of paper. He would then look at the paper and use the patterns to generate images, patterns, and associations in his head. Many of his inventions jumped into his head prompted by these scribbles.

This is not to say that the scribbles generated the ideas. It is undoubtedly the case that somewhere in his head he had all of the material necessary for generating the invention. But the scribbles provided a mechanism to jog his mind towards new associations, new combinations of thought.

TIMEOUT

■ Journey plan

The first requirement for implementation is a plan. By now we can hear virtual hair being torn from virtual heads. We've surveyed; we've generated ideas in the building phase; we've polished them in waymarking. Now we've arrived at navigating and what happens? We still don't get started on the real business at hand. Now we plan – isn't that what we've been doing in the first three stages?

In a word, no. What we've produced is an idea, an approach, a concept. But we still need to put that idea into practice. If the idea is for a new product, we need to get that new product manufactured, marketed and into the consumers' hands. If we are solving a problem, the solution needs to be applied. Whatever we are doing, navigating will generally be a multistage process.

The journey plan is the principal tool we will use. The plan is a very flexible tool. It can be anything from a handful of steps scribbled on the back of a healthfood snack bar packet (the politically correct equivalent of a cigarette packet) to a huge, detailed construct assembled in a project planning package. The choice is yours, dependent on the type of navigation and your resources. Before we plunge into the plan, though, what else do we need to pack for the journey?

■ Packing a bag

The journey plan is one essential, but there are often others. In a real, physical journey you will probably want to take money, keys, and perhaps refreshments, a portable phone, your diary, a laptop computer, any relevant documents … there's quite a list.

Similarly, on our Imagination Engineering navigation, there's some luggage we might like to consider. The first is your resource list. What and who will you need to complete your task? Are they available? What could you do to make them available?

Secondly there's that portable phone. One of the most powerful aspects of a portable is being able to make a call on the way to an appointment. Need last minute directions? Some information from the office? The cellular phone is a lifeline, providing a mechanism to call for help and get immediate assistance. In packing your bag for this particular navigation, make sure that you have your portable phone – you know how to call for assistance if things are going wrong – and you have your phone book – you know who to call and how to contact them.

■ Tracking

Once the journey is underway, you will normally want to track what is happening. On a real journey, this can be a complex process. Tracking pulls together time and action. Unless your journey is purely for enjoyment, an end in itself, your principal aim will be to reach your destination by a predetermined time. If you are taking a ten minute drive to work, this will probably be all that you consider. If, however, you are making a longer journey you will usually have checkpoints along the way.

Baggage

Try your hand at our metaphor. We identify below what the portable phone is; what might correspond to the refreshments or the keys?

Tracking

Check out the three most important things you're working on right now. What is the next milestone for each?

These might be principal places that you will pass through, or simply convenient distances measured on a milestone. In either case, you will be able to see how you are doing against your journey plan and take appropriate action – speed up, change route, alert your destination – if you are going astray.

For a very long journey, these intermediate milestones take on the nature of destinations in their own right. An obvious example is a round-the-world cruise. Say you set off from the English port, Southampton: your destination is Southampton, in itself not the most exciting prospect, but the intermediate destinations are much more significant. Even if your final destination is critically important, on long journeys you will need intermediate destinations. People like to arrive in a comfortable timescale – it's not always enough to know that you will get somewhere in five years' time.

As we look at the navigation process, we should always be searching for appropriate milestones along the way.

■ Arriving

If you are the only one involved in your navigation, it may well be enough to bask in the warm glow of success. If, however, there are others involved, it is worth marking the arrival. This has a multiple function. There's a strong human desire for rites of passage, clearly establishing a change of status. Completing the implementation of a significant idea or the solution of a major problem deserves equal recognition.

You may also need to publicize the completion, whether for pure marketing reasons or for indirect marketing – to sell to your clients the fact that you really do deliver. Whether or not this is the case, it will often be sensible to mark and celebrate an arrival with those involved.

 **Circular logic**
Think of another undertaking where the end destination is less significant than the interim stages.

 Arriving
What's your next big deliverable? Have you planned to celebrate it? How could you do so?

 **TIMEOUT**

Creativity blockers – it's not logical, Captain

We value logic highly. The Star Trek character Mr Spock was valued for his logic above all else. In some episodes it led him astray where emotions were involved, but in most cases it would bring him to the right path. The problem with logic is that it works only as well as the initial premises which frame the problem. If the question is asked in the wrong way then no amount of logic will find the best answer.

Experience will lead us to frame questions in a particular way. This is the same experience which has made it difficult for us to find a solution in the first place. In order to find a creative solution we must start outside the limitations of logic and only when we have moved into a new area, work our way back. The techniques in this book are aimed at making that process easier.

■ Flexible or check box?

For a long time there has been a single acceptable approach to implementation in business. Coming out of vast engineering and building projects, the "waterfall" approach requires the production of an extremely detailed project plan with linked interdependencies and resource requirements identified and pinned down. As the implementation proceeds, those involved can (and do) spend endless happy hours charting progress to the nth degree and making sure that there is a good culprit when things go wrong, as they often do.

"As they often do" is the give-away. The title "project" ought to warn us. A project is a planned undertaking, one where the planners project their plans into the future. Sadly, the real world is not hugely amenable to human planning. The number of variables beyond our control is simply too large to make accurate predictions of what is going to happen. This is especially true when we are dealing with not only the (relatively) simple components of physical objects but also the more complex matrix of feelings and experience which control human responses.

This all sounds very depressing. It seems that planning is a hopeless exercise and that we have to launch out on our journey unprepared and open to disaster. In practice things aren't quite so bad. For a large project where human and natural considerations have relatively limited impact, traditional project planning is reasonably effective. In other circumstances another approach is needed. We recommend considering this second, flexible approach as the standard way to plan an implementation, holding back the traditional approach and its heavyweight tools for those exercises where it is necessary.

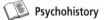 **Psychohistory**

In the 1950s, science fiction writer Isaac Asimov pictured a science which would predict future history by applying statistical methods to the behavior of people (see *Foundation*, etc.). Thankfully, current mathematics suggests that such accuracy of prediction is impossible.

■ A flexible friend

In fact, the approach we suggest for navigation is not new; it has been applied to one particular aspect of implementation for a long time. The novelty is in applying it widely, though even this is becoming more commonplace as businesses like software development come to realize that conventional development approaches simply aren't working.

The flexible approach takes the methods used by product designers, whether working on a car radio or the car itself, to come up with an acceptable new product. Underlying the implementation approach are two fundamentals – prototyping and rapid iteration in fixed timescales.

In conventional planning, having decided what we want to achieve we go through a lengthy phase of agreeing detailed specifications with the supplier and the client. The benefit of this conventional approach for the supplier is twofold – they can avoid problems when the client changes their mind part way through the implementation, and they can have a cast iron set of milestones against which to check off progress. With every box ticked, the implementation is successfully completed, even if the end-product is something that no-one wants or uses.

From the client's viewpoint, they have a stick to hold over their supplier to ensure that exactly what was asked for is delivered. Sadly, though, the client rarely knows exactly what they do want. If we are implementing an idea generated by creativity techniques we may well be dealing with a concept which does not fit easily with common experience. How, then, can we specify at the outset exactly what is needed?

With the flexible approach, this is not necessary. The flexible implementation has a maximum of four simple phases which provide the milestones for the development. These are: the concept clarifier, the demonstrator, the working subset and the final product.

If the idea is very new, the concept clarifier is used first. This does not even attempt to be a working model of the final solution, it is a picture of what might be, of the sort of result which can be expected. A crude simulation of the idea (typically these days on a computer) is used as a communication device to enable those who are to make

Recipe for disaster
This is rather like expecting the clientele of a restaurant to specify exactly what goes into a dish, down to the quantity of each spice, before they eat it.

Concept clarifier
What might a concept clarifier for a new designer water sport be like?

the decisions understand what is being proposed and give their feedback. When a computer company was developing a pen tablet, i.e. a thin, lightweight device like a slate which can be written on with a pen, the concept clarifier weighed 45 pounds and filled a large briefcase. It bore no resemblance to the finished product, but gave an idea of what it might do.

The demonstrator is more of a working model. This gives the impression of acting like a subset of the actual product or solution, though it may be based on a totally different working premise. This could be a dumb mock-up, like the traditional models of cars, or a computer simulation which looks and feels like the real thing.

In the next stage, the actual approach is used, but on the minimum subset of the task which is necessary to get value from the outcome. This stage produces something a true customer can use as it is designed to be used, but it will not perform all the tasks which it will finally have to cover.

Finally the finishing touches are put in place. At each of these four stages the deliverables are put in the hands of the final users. Feedback from those users – whether they are consumers of a new type of food or staff trying out a new pay scheme – is crucial to the effective implementation. It is much easier to describe this approach in terms of physical objects, but the flexible plan can apply equally to an intangible idea or problem. The concept clarifier could be a description of a new way of pricing, or better, a computer program which applies this pricing strategy to your portfolio. Even a one-off construction like a building is amenable to this approach if the right sort of people are involved. The demonstrator may well be a computer model. The minimum subset requires a different approach to construction but it is possible.

It is not necessary to plan out in intricate detail what will go into an implementation if the flexible approach is taken. In fact it would be pointless, as each stage will change the nature of the following one. However, the danger with a prototyping approach is infinite refinement – the desire to keep going back and make one more improvement before the implementation is complete.

For this reason, the prototyping approach must always be accompanied by tight time boxing to ensure true flexibility. This means for

Philips

The electronics giant uses software called RAPRO-T to create mock-ups of new products in great detail.

Working subset

What would you envisage a working subset of a public transport system for a large city to be? Has your nearest city even achieved this?

Working subset

"A complex system that works is invariably found to have evolved from a simple system that worked. A complex system designed from scratch never works and cannot be made to work. You have to start over, beginning with a working system."
(John Gall, *Systemantics* (New York Times Book Company, 1977))

each stage, and potentially each iteration within the stage, a fixed timing is allowed. While there can be negotiation along the way to trade off the amount of time allowed, the overall time boxes are considered sacrosanct.

This flexibility sounds great, but how are the timescales arrived at? There is no better means of coming up with timescales than reverting to the basics of a check box approach. But the big difference is that the detailed plan is thrown away once time boxes are agreed on – it is definitely a fiction, so why measure against it? Also, the plan will not need to cover so much detail in the first place, anything more than a couple of sheets of paper is probably too detailed.

Is this the approach for your particular implementation? Quite probably. The best introduction is to build a broad-brush traditional plan (see next section), then see whether you can adopt a flexible style. The biggest deciding factor will be the people involved. To make a flexible implementation work, they need to be self-starters, focussed on delivery, they need to be motivated and wanting to achieve what you want to do. If the people involved aren't like this you need to do two things: use a conventional check box implementation; and start work on a new project – how to get new people.

Time is money
There is an interesting side effect of this approach. Conventionally, companies have measured effort (and rewarded) by time, not tasks. Taking a time boxing approach means that the number of hours worked and when they are worked is much more under the individual's control. This tends to make for a more satisfied workforce and strongly supports the move towards more flexible working methods and increased individual responsibility.

TIMEOUT

Misunderstanding – Electron microscopes

The modern electron microscope was developed by a physicist who had heard of but not seen such a microscope. He worked out three theoretical approaches, one of which was superior to the approach which had been developed.

■ Everything checks

The previous section has given check box implementation a hard time. But remember, even the flexible approach needs some broad-brush check box planning, and you may not be in a position to manage a flexible implementation right now. The first thing to do is to check out your needs:

- What you want to do
- Why you want to do it

- Where you want to do it
- How you are going to do it
- When you should start and finish
- What resources are needed – people and others
- How you will get help if things go wrong

Many of the answers to these questions will already have been garnered in the earlier stages of Imagination Engineering, but a good start to the planning process is to pull those answers together.

With these answers in front of you, draw out a high level task list. Split the "what" answer down into a set of discrete tasks which need to be completed. Some of these will act as milestones along the way in a check box implementation, or as breaks in the time boxes in a flexible approach.

By putting a finger in the air and delving into your own experience (or someone else's if they've done this sort of task more often), put broad timings against these tasks. Fit these timings to a calendar, bearing in mind the limitations of non-productive time.

By this stage you've got as much of a plan together as you'll probably need for the flexible approach. If you wish or need to continue with the check box approach and you are dealing with a regimented, complex implementation (and you should ask yourself why you are using a check box approach if you haven't got a regimented, complex implementation) you will then need to move on to the next level of detail.

There was a time when this would involve drawing lots of painfully crafted diagrams. We would no longer expect this from a planner any more than we would expect an engineer to pull out a slide rule when faced with a calculation. Project management software takes much of the tedious drawing and calculating out of detailed project planning (though nothing can take away the tedium of entering data and monitoring it). If you need to go to the next level of detail, move to such a package.

Software packages come and go, but there is a good range of products available to support the planner. Until recently there was a big divide between cheap and cheerful packages from the traditional software houses, which were big on usability and low on functionality, and high power packages from consultancies and specialist

Slide rules and valves

Slide rules illustrate the difficulties of doing more than broad-brush planning. It was assumed in the 1960s that the slide rule would continue to be a common engineer's tool. Similarly, the excellent science fiction writer James Blish wrote a piece which was based on the assumption that radio and computers could not be used near to Jupiter – because the gravity is so high that valves would implode. Oops.

houses, which could cope with much bigger problems but were as user-friendly as a brick on the head. Now the products are much closer together in terms of functionality and usability, with only the outrageous variation in pricing clearly identifying the backgrounds.

HOW TO PUT IT TOGETHER

■ What type of journey?

Navigating is particularly dependent on external factors. Although the broad toolkit remains the same, we have identified four principal types of journey – types of problem or idea generation – which you are liable to have to cope with. Each of the journey types will make different calls on your navigating toolkit.

The railway

On a train you know where you want to go, the train itself has a clear set of destinations and the driving is left to someone else. Even the driver has limited control over the journey – he can't suddenly turn off the tracks and divert into a field (at least, not without an accompanying disaster). The railway is an implementation where all the details are left to someone else. You set the destination, but after that will be content with updates on progress and reaching milestones. A railway implementation will be contracted out or severely delegated. Of itself, the railway does not demand either a flexible or a check box approach – the decision on which direction to take is more likely to depend on the capabilities of the person doing the driving for you. Milestones, whether within the formal plan or as breakpoints in the time boxes, will be very important to you. Your lack of active involvement will demand greater concentration on these key points.

The highway

The highway has some similarities to the railway. There are distinct starting and stopping places – you can't leave the highway wherever you would like. But now you are in the driving seat. You control the speed and the routing. You decide when to leave the highway. The highway is a simple implementation under your own control. The

Railways
Although England's Stockton and Darlington Railway, opened in 1825, was technically the first public steam railway, the Liverpool and Manchester Railway (1830) was the first to carry both passengers and freight and to be worked entirely by steam. George Stephenson was the principal engineer in both cases.

Highways
The German autobahns of the 1930s effectively defined the modern highway or motorway.

destination is clear, the implementation straightforward, though it may be very long and have many stages and people involved.

The highway is the best suited of the four journey types to the traditional check box approach. It may be, even if a journey is not a true highway, that you have to act as if it were and enforce a check box approach because those involved cannot cope with any other sort of implementation. Unfortunately by treating a country lane as a highway you will get many more unexpected hazards, which your rigid plan will find difficult to respond to. Think of trying to drive a car down a twisty, single track road with the cruise control set to highway speeds – the analogy works horribly well.

The country lane

Examined at the level of the basic elements used to construct it there is no real difference between navigating a country lane and a highway. But in practice they are worlds apart. Driving down a country lane can be much more fun – but equally it's much easier to get caught behind a tractor and become frustrated. A country lane bends and twists, often concealing your destination, and getting from A to B through country lanes requires much more concentration. The opportunities to branch off and get lost are endless, but so are the chances to be flexible and take an alternate route through the network of tiny roads if your original ideas become blocked.

When the implementation is of this type you will need much more direction in the implementation. Tracking is required along the way. You simply won't be able to put together a detailed plan ahead of time – the flexible approach has a lot going for it here.

The river

A river is vastly different from any of the previous, man-made routes. Here external forces play a huge part in determining your direction and speed. The journey will typically be much slower, with more possibilities for stopping off along the way. Such an implementation will often apply either to personal goals or the fundamental, long-term direction of a company, rather than day-to-day operations.

Once more, flexibility will come into play because the sheer timescales involved make detailed planning next to impossible.

Country lanes

Many explanations have been provided for the intricate windings of country lanes, typified by those of the English county of Cornwall. Though some have described them following lines of force in the ground and others suggest that the curves were designed to prevent build-ups of snow, most are following ancient field boundaries.

Rivers

The longest river in the world, the Nile, runs 6,741 kilometers from Burundi to the Mediterranean sea.

■ What's what?

It's rather easy to get lost in navigation, as any frustrated map reader will know. In practice, the process is very simple: decide what sort of navigation you are undertaking; draw up a simple plan; convert that, as appropriate, into a flexible plan or a check box plan; make sure you've packed your mobile phone to call for help; and set off, checking the milestones as you go.

Classifying the type of navigation is not essential, but it helps you to move forward with a clearer idea of what is necessary. To help you get a feel for these classifications, here are a handful of navigation exercises. You will identify what sort of navigation is underway, then experience part of the actual process.

What sort of navigation
Which category does the most important task you are currently undertaking fit into?

TIMEOUT

Einstein

Most people know that Albert Einstein did not initially develop the general theory of relativity at a desk or a blackboard but while lying on a hill on a summer's day. As he looked up with half-closed eyes, according to his own account, the sun dappled through his eyelashes, breaking into thousands of tiny beams. He wondered what it would be like to go for a ride on one of those sun beams and imagined himself taking a journey through the Universe.

His imaginary trip took a form that was entirely wrong according to the physics and mathematics of the day. Trusting in his imagination, he worked at the problem and in the process developed a new form of mathematics which explained his journey.

Navigation 1: The move

Medical International Group has faced up to the fact that its private hospital site in the center of a busy city is no longer suitable. An opportunity has arisen to move to a much cheaper, much more accessible site, raising enough funds to build a brand new, shiny hospital twice the size of the current facility.

This idea, generated by using Imagination Engineering, now needs implementing. As navigator, which type of implementation would you choose?

Planning questions
See p. 99.

Don't read on until you've thought through the four options – railway, highway, lane or river. We want you to fix them firmly in your mind.

Okay. This is in all probability a highway implementation. Building projects are among the best for quantifying to small detail the aspects involved, and legislation limits the flexibility you can put into the design of a hospital. This looks like a check box implementation of a highway.

As an exercise, spend five minutes outlining the principal questions for your plan. Can't remember what they are? Check back. We could ask you to take this a stage further and set up the plan in a project management package, but your time is precious, and we aren't that cruel.

Navigation 2: The whites of their eyes

You are the regional manager of a cut-price firm of opticians. Your closest rival has opened an outlet directly facing yours in a shopping mall. Your problem is how to keep your revenue, faced with such direct opposition. A creativity session has come up with a strategy of relationship marketing. You will move from a passive shop which has no real relationship with its customers, to an active business which seems to know each of its customers individually.

There are difficulties in this, of course. You have in the past differentiated yourselves from the old-fashioned opticians by a move to a more supermarket-like feel. You need to make your customers feel special without scaring them off. There are a number of suggestions to help achieve this. The whole scheme needs to be showing results by the time of your career review in six months, or you will be looking for a new job.

This is more of a country lane. You are in the very unpleasant position of having to try radical changes without a clear plan. This problem is also ideally suited to taking a flexible approach. Until you start to get some response from customers, you can't really be sure what they will respond to. Assuming that the basic idea itself is sound, enabling you to skip over concept clarifier and demonstrator stages,

For real
This example actually took place in a local shopping mall. So far, the remedy has been a price war: unless one or other of the opticians comes up with a more creative solution, they may not have a very happy future.

sketch out time boxes for a minimum working subset and full implementation. You have six months overall and should allow for three iterations in the subset phase and two in the full phase. Remember to do a quick sketch task list to work out what your time boxes should look like.

Navigation 3: From square one

You are starting a small business from scratch. This is not a short-term venture: you intend to stay with it for the next 10 to 20 years. We've already met the business in the waymarking section: it's the PC doctor service, where you will offer a support service to home-based PC users. Which category might this fall in?

This we see as a river implementation. Although the short-term aspects of setting up the company may well require a highway to carry them through, the overall plan for the company is long term and broad.

As an exercise, assuming your actual destination is to be able to retire in ten years' time with enough money in the bank to have no further financial worries, set yourself a number of time box milestones, initially every three months, then annually from two years.

Navigation 4: Teaching teacher

Educational establishments have long argued over the rights and wrongs of teacher assessment. As head of an autonomous school, it is up to you to implement a performance oriented pay scheme for your teachers over the next year to improve teaching quality. What sort of implementation do you see this as?

We see it as another country lane. While improving quality as a broad goal is a river, the implementation of a performance-related pay scheme has to have specific, short timescales to prevent it from upsetting and disillusioning staff.

Ask yourself the key questions about the scheme. Think about how you could prototype the scheme. How could you take a prototyping approach with as complex a people problem as a pay scheme? We would argue, how could you *not* prototype such a scheme? What form could concept clarifiers and demonstrators take?

Personal development
What are your own long-term plans?

Navigation 5: Organizing the moaners

Your corporate spends a lot of money dealing with customer complaints, currently handled in a messy, manual process. You would like to computerize the handling of customer complaints, but your creativity session has generated the idea of getting a third party firm to produce the system. If everything goes satisfactorily with the implementation, you may ask the same company to take over the running of your customer service department. Implementation type?

This is a pretty clear railway implementation. What milestones and measures along the way would you use? Does using a third party developer force you into a check box approach? How could you work a flexible development with a contractor? How would you decide whether or not the contractor was suitable to take over customer complaint handling?

Navigation 6: Adding the rainbow touch

Your manufacturing company is a mid-range player in all the standard, large white goods products from washing machines to fridges. You want to expand and have decided to try to create a new category of small white goods products, aimed at the same disposable income bracket as phones and CD players. To do this, the product has to be exciting (never traditionally true of white goods) and appeal more to the impulse buyer. A creativity session has generated a couple of dozen possible new products. The waymarking phase has highlighted the top five possibles. Now it's time to get serious. What style of navigation?

It's another country lane. It's not clear from the above information just how radical these ideas are. Let's assume they're sufficiently new that people don't know they want one (the Walkman is a good example of a product like this). Rough out time boxes for concept clarifiers through to production. Don't worry about timescales, unless you are actually in this business, just get a feel for what you think is needed.

Navigation exercises: Postscript

In setting up these exercises we intended to provide a balanced set of

White goods
A general term for the boring end of consumer durables which were traditionally encased in white enamel: ovens, washing machines, refrigerators and the like.

options. While we did venture into each navigation type, the country lane dominated. It's probably fair to say that the majority of navigations are actually country lanes, even if convenience or necessity drives us into using other modes.

TIMEOUT

Creativity blockers – following the rules

We said earlier that good kids conform and bad kids break the rules. The problem with rules is that they become so pervasive that they begin to create themselves. The first reaction to many creative solutions is, "but that's cheating" because those making the allegation have limited their thinking and the solution falls outside those limits. It is only after a logical path back to the starting position is developed that the cheating allegation will go away.

We have often used the training example – think of uses for a paper clip. When you tell people after the exercise that the paper clip can be made of anything they want, can be as large or small as they want, and can be processed in any way they want, they usually become annoyed. The reaction is, "you should have told us that before we started." The fact is we never told them that this was not the case. Any limitation which was placed on them was placed by themselves. This is true of any blocks to creative thinking. The blocks are self-imposed in an unconscious attempt to follow the rules.

Coming soon ➤➤➤

You've had a lot thrown at you, so we've reached a good point for a recap. After the tale piece you will find a map of Imagination Engineering – a diagram which pulls together the four aspects of the framework.

Key words

Implementation; portable phones (help!); flexible or check box plans; railway; highway; country lane; river.

Brian Martin

Has written several serious detective novels. *Deceptive Appearances* is the first chapter of an unpublished novel with a lighter slant.

DECEPTIVE APPEARANCES

By Brian Martin

The sunlight streaming through the small windows of the Old House restaurant seemed unnecessarily brash. This was an establishment where the diners spoke in whispers, an eating place with an atmosphere more appropriate for a church than a commercial enterprise. It was hard to say what induced this air of reverence in the clientele. Perhaps it was the heavy table linen and the dark, rich wallpaper. Perhaps it was the elegant, hand-written menus. Most likely it was the insufferable air of superiority displayed by all the staff, but brought to the level of an art form by the headwaiter.

When the scream came, it was all the more shocking for that hushed ambience. A woman at a nearby table knocked over her wine glass and began mopping frenziedly at the resultant pool. A middle-aged man dropped his pudding spoon. He seemed less cowed by the place. As he strained to pick up the spoon, hampered by the breadth of his paunch, an appreciative smile graced his face. The smile of a connoisseur. He did not have long to wait.

A young waiter was first on the scene. He seemed uncertain of what to do, a rare circumstance for a member of staff at that establishment. The young woman who had screamed was standing up, her chair thrown over by the force of her jump away from the table. She was shaking, pointing wordlessly at her licorice-dotted ice cream, the signature dish of the Old House chef. The waiter cleared his throat, taking advantage of the moment's delay to observe the diner. He had not noticed her before, though he was surprised at this oversight. Not so much because she was exceedingly pretty – which she was – but thanks to her appearance, deeply unusual for an Old House customer.

Her hair, somewhat over shoulder length and blonde, had a startling purple streak down the centre. Her jeans were torn in three places. Her blouse stopped just above her navel and was bright pink. Her ears were pierced in half a dozen places, garnished with a mixed salad of cheap jewellery. And, he noticed, she had brown, bare feet, her nails embellished with a carmine polish. It was, he thought, quite amazing that she had been allowed entrance in the first place, though it was lunch and these days you had to accept anything at lunch. Even trainers and leggings. It was the American influence, he supposed. Despite only being in his early twenties, he held very old-fashioned views.

"Does madam need something?" he asked, deciding that he could no longer justify silently staring at her.

She noticed him for the first time. Her big, brown eyes widened. "Thank goodness," she said. "There's a slug in my ice cream."

"A slug?" said the young waiter uncertainly. "In your ice cream?"

"That's it." She pointed to one of the larger pieces of licorice, which obligingly twitched and sprouted a pair of horns.

"Just …" the waiter did not know what to do. He fought a hysterical urge to inform her that it would hardly eat much. "I'll bring the headwaiter. Please don't … Just …" With this concise instruction he disappeared into the kitchen.

Guillaume, the headwaiter, sailed majestically across the restaurant floor a few moments later. There was no trace of surprise or distress in his expression. He might have been carved from stone. "Yes?" he said curtly as he arrived at the table. "Mademoiselle?"

"In my ice cream," repeated the young woman. "A slug."

"A slug," said Guillaume slowly. He bent forward stiffly to examine her plate more closely, removing his small-rimmed spectacles and peering through one of the lenses with a squinting eye, as if he were an Edwardian detective. "A slug," Guillaume straightened stiffly. "Where did it come from?"

"I'm sorry?" said the young woman. "How should I know? It's a slug, not a bus, it doesn't come with a route map."

"And you allege that this slug was delivered on your ice cream?" Guillaume's tone was sad, as if he had caught a beloved child lying.

"It was," said the young woman. "That's how it came."

"I see," said Guillaume. "Let me paint you a picture. Imagine a young woman who desires a good lunch, but has not the wherewithal to pay. Perhaps she might know that the Old House is famous for her licorice ice. Perhaps she might bring a slug with her, slip it into the pudding and then cry out to the embarrassment of the management. Might that not be so?"

"I don't know what you mean," said the young woman. Her lower lip trembled briefly.

"Of course you don't," said Guillaume. "And I don't …"

"Excuse me." It was the portly, middle-aged man. "A moment, please." The waiter turned quickly, anger momentarily distorting his face, but he could not ignore the authority of that voice.

"Yes, sir?"

"I couldn't help notice what is happening." The big man grinned. He seemed to be enjoying himself. "I saw the young lady's pudding arrive." He beckoned the headwaiter closer. "I noticed it myself. Frankly, she's not the sort I'd allow in the place, but she is telling the truth. The slug was on board when the ice cream landed."

Guillaume blinked, such was the extreme nature of his emotions. He walked stiffly back to the other table, taking the few steps with careful precision. "I gather, mademoiselle, that I accused you falsely. We will, of course, forget any charges. And I will replace your ice cream, or bring you any other dessert."

"Thank you," said the young woman, "but I'd rather not." She took a deep breath. "I'm going now."

"As you will, mademoiselle," said Guillaume, walking her to the door. "I hope we will have the pleasure of your company again."

The woman did not reply, but as she passed through the door she turned and gave Guillaume a smile of such power that even his frozen lips twitched in reply. He watched her from the door for a moment, then returned to the table of the middle-aged diner.

"I am so sorry, sir," he said.

"It is shocking," said the middle-aged man. "Shocking."

Guillaume looked carefully, but there was not a hint of sarcasm in the man's expression. "Yes, sir," he said.

"I've been coming here for twenty years," said the middle-aged man. "Mostly in the old days before your time. Wouldn't have happened then, when the restaurant first opened. Never seen anything like it. A slug; remarkable."

"I am so sorry," said Guillaume again. He had been about to remark on the diner's lack of familiarity, but felt undermined by such longevity of custom. "You will do me the honour of accepting your lunch on the house?"

"That's very kind," said the middle-aged man. "I'll have a coffee and a glass of ten-year-old Tawny before I go."

It was fifteen minutes later that he emerged onto the pavement, blinking as the full force of the summer sun glinted on his shiny forehead. He tapped the board by the door with the umbrella he always carried, even in the heat of midsummer, running the point along the elegantly simple words "Old House" and the establishment date. His expression was positively jovial as he started down the street.

It said a lot for the middle-aged man's equilibrium that he did not stop walking when a young woman – *the* young woman – leaped from a narrow side-alley, flung her arms around his neck, and kissed him. He broke step, it is true, but little more than a hesitation and a raised eyebrow marked her arrival.

"Thank you," she said, forcing her arms around his waist. "My hero."

"Do I know you?" the middle-aged man enquired.

"The old fogey thought I was lying."

"Guillaume. The headwaiter is called Guillaume. Frankly I wouldn't have believed you in his position."

"Not until I was bailed out by an eye-witness." She patted him on the back. "Did you see me put the slug on the ice cream?"

The middle-aged man shook his head. "In that you were discretion itself."

"From you, Anthony, that's more than a compliment. I trust you got a free meal out of them too."

"I did, though it was touch and go for a moment. He obviously wondered how he'd missed such a regular customer. My information is out of date; I had him down as a new man."

"That was the evening maitre de," said the young woman.

"Of course, Wendy, you're right." Anthony scanned the street appreciatively. "And, flattering though it is, I would appreciate it if you detached yourself from me. People will get the wrong idea."

"We wouldn't want that." But she kept her arm around his waist.

"No, really," said Anthony. "They might think we were like those two." He pointed across the street to another couple, arm-in-arm outside the display windows of W.H. Smith's. The woman must have been fifty, though she was well preserved. Her companion, a wild looking young man, was no more than half her age.

"Ugh," said Wendy. "How grotesque." She untwined her arm, bit her lip thoughtfully, then threaded her way through the traffic towards the offending couple. Anthony followed casually behind. As Wendy came closer she could see that the woman was expensively dressed. Smart but understated. "Baby sitting, are you?" Wendy said bluntly. "Did he need someone to hold his hand?"

"Absolutely," said the older woman. "Here you are, have him back." She pushed the young man in Wendy's direction. "How did you get on, Anthony? They were suspicious at our place. They let Ben off, but I had to pay for my own lunch."

"Shocking," said Anthony. "What are things coming to?"

"Four lunches for the price of one isn't bad, Laura," said Wendy.

"It's the principle of the thing," said the older woman. "I hate it when someone doesn't trust me."

"There, there," said Anthony, putting his hand on her shoulder. "Mean pickings here, team. I don't think Taunton's for us. I hear that Dunster is a tasty spot. I suggest we adjourn to there, put up in a decent hotel and consider our options. Cash is running low – we've got some work to do."

"Let's go to the West Country for a holiday, you said," grumbled Ben.

"No rest for the wicked," said Wendy, taking her husband's hand. "Anyone for a spot of shopping before we go? It's ages since I've played the Marks and Spencer returns game."

 Sympathetic rogues

Martin's dubious characters are inspired by those in the delightful *Ways and Means* by the now neglected author Henry Cecil. Other sympathetic rogues to grace the crime scene are E. W. Hornung's classic *Raffles* and Jonathan Gash's *Lovejoy*, whose literary exploits tend to be significantly less heroic than his popular TV persona.

Key thoughts

- There's a fine line between cheating and creativity
- Actually there's no line at all
- Creativity should be fun
- There is such a thing as a free lunch.

IMAGINATION ENGINEERING – THE MAP

Surveying

The survey is where we establish our destination and surroundings, noting factors which may influence the decision or problem area. A known destination can be checked with the compass. If there is no clear goal, the level chain is ideal.

- **Compass** – Question stated directions. Ask "why?"
- **Obstacle map** – Identify blockages.
- **Level chain** – Find new destinations by moving up and down levels.
- **Aerial survey** – Collect information. Overview. Mind map.
- **Destination** – The problem is stated as "How to get to ...?"

Building

The building stage overcomes problems and obstacles on the way to a solution. Typically one or two techniques might be employed for a particular obstacle.

- **Tunnel** – Techniques which push through the obstacle. Challenging assumptions; distortion of facts; reversal of relationships.
- **Bridge** – Techniques that look at the problem from a different direction. Indulging in fantasy; taking the view of a different person or time; applying a metaphor.
- **By-pass** – Using a secondary destination to get around the blockage. Random word or picture, objects and nonsense.
- **New destination** – Sometimes it is more effective to go to another destination altogether. Second best solution.

Waymarking

When the route is established we need to mark the way, refining and clarifying. The waymarking stage may generate some extra building. Waymarking can be a private or public exercise to gather a range of views.

- **Slip road** – Slimming down possible solutions.
- **Washroom** – A purely subjective judgement: what do you feel about it?
- **Viewpoints** – Considering all stakeholders' views.
- **Signposts** – Looking at everything that's good.
- **Hazard markers** – Looking at what's wrong with the idea and suggesting ways to fix it.

Navigating

...aving established the practicality of the idea ...d tuned it, it needs to be put into practice. ...fferent navigation approaches are available ...r different types of problem.

- **The highway** – Where there is an obvious path and a detailed plan would be more obstacle than help. Requires a clear goal and few, broadly stated, milestones. There are slip roads to cope with changes due to outside influence.
- **The country lane** – Where there is no obvious path and more flexible planning is needed, the country lane provides the opportunity to think through each stage of the journey individually.
- **The railway** – Someone else is driving, but you will still keep track of progress. Agree route and stations to monitor progress against.
- **The river** – Very long-term goals, where the journey is daunting. This can only be achieved by rowing one stroke at a time, but holding in mind the destination.

INSTITUTIONALIZING CREATIVITY

- Organized or disorganized resistance
- Listening to yourself
- Listening to others
- Valuing difference
- Creating and maintaining teams
- Conflict between step change and internal entrepreneurs
- Taking risks
- Personal acts of rebellion
- Leadership
- Facilitators
- Role models
- Institutional safety valves

ORGANIZED OR DISORGANIZED
RESISTANCE

Metaphor

The resistance metaphor was created at dinner with Henry Berry of Theory B – "Ideation Consultants". Dinner is a great place not to do too much business.

The metaphor that we are going to use for this section is that of resistance to an oppressor. It feels like that in a large organization at times. You want desperately to change the way the organization works, but there is an invisible hand redirecting things back the way they have always been. Often the oppressor is not the person in charge. Indeed, you may be the boss, searching for ways to make things change. At times it is hard to see where this organizational power for inertia emanates from. Everybody wants things to be different, yet nothing changes. Often, those same people who are complaining about the way an organization works are the ones who are perpetuating the very substance of their complaints. An unacceptable level of inertia often feels more comfortable than even a small amount of change.

What is needed is a resistance movement, an army of liberation working for the organization but fighting against the inbuilt tendency to inhibit energy, creativity and fun. It's an important point that the resistance comes from within. The French Resistance in the Second World War were not fighting against France. A creativity underground is not fighting against the organization, it is fighting against the oppressor – the invisible hand which supports inertia and stifles creativity.

The French Resistance

Perhaps the most famous underground liberation movement is the French Resistance Army of the Second World War. Fighting against the rule of the Germans and Vichy, their opponent was more tangible than the opponent of a creativity underground.

Should resistance be organized or disorganized? You can act as a one person army, fighting your own war with no support, but you will be more effective working with others. There is something apparently contradictory about organizing a resistance movement if you have some power in the organization. That is why it is necessary to understand that an organization is rarely led by its leaders, rather it is led by its expectations of the future. The role of the leader is to shape those expectations. There is an important point here. Most who fight against inertia see it as being driven by the past. It is not. It is driven by the expectation that tomorrow will be more or less like today. Once you truly believe that tomorrow will be different, your actions will change in line with your expectations.

This is not to say that the past cannot have a significant effect – in the worst organizations, expectations are rigidly moulded by an obsessive desire to maintain the status quo – but it remains the view of the future which leads us on. Look at the importance placed on hope, the dream of betterment that has shaped Western society. It's expectations that count.

LISTENING TO YOURSELF

Whether you are part of an army or a lone soldier, remember that an organization is a collection of individuals. It may behave differently to any one of the individuals within it, but it is driven by what they think, believe and do. As one of the individuals in your organization, you can make a difference to the way it behaves. The more influence you have, the more opportunity you have to alter the views of others and to set their expectations, but even if you work in the post room you have no excuse for disowning the culture of your organization. You are a part of it.

If the messages in this book make sense to you, if you believe that your organization could become more creative, you can and should do something about it. Listen to yourself and make sure you like what you hear. Decide to be a role model for the way you would like things to be. Act differently. Be seen as different. You will make a difference. Then again, you might get fired; no-one said creativity was always easy.

A useful, perhaps even a necessary enabling tool for anyone who wants to listen to themselves is assertiveness. Assertiveness is not, as some believe, a vehicle for manipulating those around you. Think of being assertive as helping you to decide how to live your own life. This book cannot cover the subject of assertiveness in a meaningful way, it takes at least a whole book and probably a great deal more to do that.

Another useful tool for someone who wishes to influence an organization's culture, is arrogance. Not the sort of arrogance which refuses to listen to or acknowledge the views of others, but a faith in yourself and a willingness to stand alone (if only for a short while). At the very heart of creativity, and requiring this brand of arrogance,

 The status quo

A brilliant evocation of the desire to maintain the status quo is provided by Jonathan Lynn and Antony Jay, *The Complete Yes Minister and Yes Prime Minister* (BBC Books, 1984) where the driving force behind the civil service is resisting change.

 Assertiveness

A useful book on assertiveness is Manuel J. Smith, *When I say No I feel Guilty* (Bantam, 1975).

Juggling

If you fancy trying your hand at it, we recommend John Cassidy and B.C. Rimbeaux, *Juggling for the Complete Klutz* (Klutz Press, 1988) or, for a prettier approach, Lydia Darbyshire, *Juggling* (Quintet Publishing,1993).

is a willingness to make mistakes. To illustrate this, consider the apprentice juggler. It's not until the balls are being dropped that the trainee is pushing the limits of his or her ability. Having mastered one juggling technique, there is always more to learn. The best jugglers in the world drop things when pushing their limits.

Making mistakes in an organization is much the same. As long as you are delivering more than you cost, you are helping the business. It is our contention that a creative individual delivers far more than they cost. At any point in time, though, this same individual may be generating short-term costs through their mistakes. Risk making those mistakes. If your ideas are truly creative they will initially be seen as wrong whatever their value. Believe in the idea. Test this belief. Is a proposal rejected because it is new and challenging, or is it because it really was a dumb idea after all? Can you know without testing it? How much will testing the idea risk? If the greatest thing at stake is your pride, it is worth taking the gamble.

All of the things you can do creatively for your company as an individual pale into insignificance when compared with developing a culture where people say what they think. Is your organization like this? Can you say what you think without fear of affecting your future prospects? Can others? What can you do to encourage a more open culture?

TIMEOUT

Ambiguity

"Seal up the mouth of outrage for a while, Till we can clear these ambiguities."
(William Shakespeare, *Romeo and Juliet*)

Creativity blockers – removing ambiguity

Ambiguity is at the heart of many aspects of creativity: humor could not work without it; many elements of art depend on it; creative ideas rely on it. Some people are comfortable with ambiguous situations but most of us prefer to remove the ambiguity by defining the world in ever tighter spirals around ourselves. Naturally, since our knowledge of the world is imperfect, our tighter definitions contain elements of imperfection. The disadvantage of this process is not so much the removal of the ambiguity as the assumption that the path we have chosen is the way things have to be. The advantage of an ambiguous situation is that it allows for more than one possible outcome. The creative path may not yet have been closed to us.

LISTENING TO OTHERS

Unlikely though it may seem, some of the ideas above are aimed at making you a better listener. Being assertive, as opposed to aggressive, inevitably includes a notion of allowing the rights of others. It is not so clear that a small dose of arrogance can help with listening. However, the more sure you are of yourself, the less a disagreement with your views will feel like a personal attack and the more it will be an opportunity to test and refine your ideas. The requirement is enough arrogance to be sure of yourself, but not so much that you refuse to listen to others.

When apparently listening we are more often than not searching for holes in what's being said. Try listening for positives instead. When you hear an idea developing which you do not like, instead of starting to muster counter arguments, develop a habit of thinking through what's good about the argument. Once you have done that you can think about ways of taking the aspects of the idea you do not like and improving them. Treat them as obstacles to be worked on rather than reasons for rejection.

Devil's advocate

Take a subject which you feel strongly about. Now spend five minutes jotting down arguments for the opposition. Try to really feel your new viewpoint for those five minutes.

Practice at being a devil's advocate will make it easier for you to accept the validity of others' views even if you don't agree with them.

Archimedes

The Greek mathematician Archimedes is best known for leaping from his bath and running naked down the street shouting, "I've found it." Much of his work at the time was about discovering the volume of irregular shapes. It is said that during his bath he was pondering a question posed by the King about the purity of the gold in the royal crown. Realizing that the weight of water displaced in the bath would indicate the water's volume and that this could be compared with the weight of water displaced by solid gold of the same weight as the crown, he had a way of testing purity.

 **TIMEOUT**

VALUING DIFFERENCE

We are more comfortable with those who look and think like us. We tend to associate with others who share similar beliefs and who live similar lifestyles. When we are brought into close contact with others

Crazy people
Tom Peters is a burning advocate of recruiting oddballs in *The Tom Peters Seminar – Crazy Times Call for Crazy Organizations* (Macmillan, 1994).

 Shackles of perception
So often limitations are imaginary. The most common complaint among junior managers is lack of control of their budget. In itself this is rarely a real problem. The much larger problem in this example is the lack of trust in senior management. We once asked the chief executive of a corporate why he didn't allow much more local control of budgets. "We tried it," he said, "and they didn't get it right, so we pulled in the reins." That's worrying.

whose views differ radically from ours we often feel uncomfortable. Even when we do establish a friendship or a working relationship with someone who thinks very differently to us, it's easy to compartmentalize our relationship to separate the differences and stay within the area of similarity.

Organizations do this too. The biases of the people recruiting into an organization tend to select particular types of staff, those who will fit with the norms and working styles of the company. This is a good thing from the perspective of organizational continuance and in times of stability will serve a company well but most of us are not in times of stability. Perhaps it is time actively to recruit oddballs. This will be an uncomfortable process for them and for the organization. They will have a hard time fitting in. One of three things is likely to happen. Firstly, they may learn to conform. In this case you have lost little and gained little over a more obvious choice of employee. Secondly, they may leave. In this case you have lost the investment in their recruitment and any training they have undergone. Thirdly, they may change their environment to suit them. In this case you are likely to have a small but powerful enclave of creativity which could have a profound effect on your organization. We are suggesting that this possible benefit outweighs the potential cost of losing them.

CREATING AND MAINTAINING TEAMS

There is a great deal of research to support the view that effective teams thrive on difference, not similarity. This implies that the greater an organization's effectiveness at recruiting homogeneous employees, the less likely it is that they will be able to create effective teams. If you are organizing a resistance movement you also need to bear this in mind. Do not go for clones of yourself. Work on recruiting difference.

Teamwork is more than difference in the members of the team. A fundamental point which is surprisingly often overlooked is that, to be effective, the team should have a common objective. This can be difficult in a very mixed team where individuals may have their own, very different objectives. A key to success is ensuring that every one in the team knows the objective and buys into it – if necessary modifying the objective to fit the team. Once moving towards implementation, it is critical that each team member knows what is their role in making it happen.

This brings us on to the conflict between creative individuals, who need freedom to act, and the constraints of an organization. To be honest, much of this conflict is imaginary. There are situations, such as the one in the next section, where the requirements of an organization can limit the ability of its members to act, but these are less common than might be supposed. The much vaunted freedom required for creation is often unnecessary. In many creative roles, the tighter the constraints the more creative the outcome. In advertising, for instance, the complaint that a brief is too tight, too specific, is usually made by less able staff. A tight brief can drive a particularly creative response.

This is not to imply that constraints do not cause problems. It just might be, though, that the constraint is an excuse for a poor result rather than its cause.

 Institutional agenda

For more on making creativity a feature of your company see Brian Clegg's *Creativity and Innovation for Managers* (Butterworth-Heinemann, 1999).

CONFLICT BETWEEN STEP CHANGE AND INTERNAL ENTREPRENEURS

One circumstance where real conflict can occur is between a highly process driven, bureaucratic, organization and a person with an entrepreneurial character. This is particularly true during times of instability such as a step change in performance.

Within a structured organization step change requires long-term planning, it requires focus and obsessive drive. Internal entrepreneurs need flexibility. They need an organization which can change course rapidly. It seems that during times of change there is no place for entrepreneurs.

The model of change presented here is probably not the best model for times as unpredictable as ours. Today, for most change initiatives, if you have a long-term implementation plan, by the time you have finished, the world has moved on. You manage an effective implementation of a product, service or way of operating which is no longer relevant to the world.

Flexible planning
See p. 97.

A better model of change would be the approach presented in the navigation chapter. To be honest, our views are changing. In the last book we wrote, we presented a model of implementation which had long-term plans, milestones in the traditional sense and an obsessive drive to achieve. For your industry, that model may still be relevant. For most, the prototyping approach will make more sense. With this model of implementation there is not only a place for the entrepreneur, they become an essential ingredient.

TAKING RISKS

Resistance involves risk. Often that risk is more imagined than real but, make no mistake, it is there and could result in severe sanctions for those taking the risks. By the way they work and the way they organize themselves, organizations can encourage or discourage risk taking.

Killing risk taking
Write down three common practices in your organization (or business environment) which discourage risk.

Ten ways to kill risk taking in an organization

- Centralized decision making
- Committee decision making
- High formality – based on hierarchy
- Early evaluation of ideas
- Control budgets against pre-set plans
- Performance pay against pre-set plans
- Stay within departments
- Punish mistakes
- Manage by fear
- Be careful

Encouraging risk
What improvements could be made in your organization or business environment if badges of office (real or implied) were removed?

Ten ways to encourage risk taking

- Make decisions where action happens
- Reward success based on risks
- Allocate money to entrepreneurs
- Low formality
- Remove badges of office
- Remove rules
- Respect learning
- Have fun
- Many cross-departmental projects
- Trust your people

But this is not something you "do" to an organization. This is something you live, eat and breathe. If risk taking and learning through making mistakes are not exhibited and even celebrated at the top of an organization then there is no chance that they will flourish further down.

A great practical demonstration of taking risks was set up by Henry Berry of Theory B, "Ideation Consultants." He wanted to show a group of company executives the excitement that risk taking can generate. He arranged for a car to be driven to where they waited, handed them all sledgehammers and told them to destroy the car. They wouldn't begin until they were pushed, almost goaded into it. Once they had started, though, they had a wonderful time.

The feedback after the session was entirely about the fun of the experience, largely because it was perceived as a forbidden act. What they hadn't been told before the activity was that although the car was apparently in beautiful condition, it was barely roadworthy and had been bought for a song at an auction the day before. The main lesson for these company leaders was that the risk which they had been so loathe to take was the source of their enjoyment. Risk was not only something they avoided in their day-to-day lives, they stifled it in their organization too.

PERSONAL ACTS OF REBELLION

What can you get away with doing that will act as a small message to those around you? What steps towards individuality and creativity can you take now? In a large organization we have worked with there is a very old office block with corridor after corridor of uniform brown doors leading into uniform offices fitted with uniform furniture. Many people personalize their offices with potted plants and paintings. One individual has gone a step further by painting his door bright blue. Row after row of dark brown doors broken by one highly individual bright blue door. Some feel that this small act of rebellion is silly but even they are talking about it. Many wish they had done this first. Some are still wishing they had the courage to do this now. This is the sort of person you need to recruit into your army of liberation.

More rebellion
In another office block a corridor had a shelf below a blank stretch of wall. Someone put up a notice saying "This shelf is not a rubbish bin" to discourage dumping of waste paper there. A much more effective reply appeared a few days later: "This wall is not a window." Logical, yet funny, it puts the original notice in its place.

LEADERSHIP

Like implementation, there are conflicting views on the best ways to exhibit leadership. Not surprisingly, given our view on risk taking, we believe that good leadership involves a high degree of trust and flexibility. Creative leaders are actually collaborators with the resistance movement. They are in a position of power yet supporting those who seek to undermine a source of that power – inertia.

There are two types of people in this world. Those who divide people into two types and those who do not. There are two types of manager. Those who believe that staff are inherently out to have as easy a time as possible and those who do not. If a manager believes that their staff are not trying to do the best possible job they can, then they can never get them to be as flexible and creative as they might be.

In a creative world direction is still needed; crystal clear direction driven by an overriding vision. In a creative world huge flexibility is also needed; flexibility for people to do what they think best in order to serve the needs of their company. These needs are not contradictory.

A leader in a creative world has to provide clear direction and facilitate flexible working. Staff need to understand clearly the direction and purpose of their company but they need to be allowed to follow these with latitude to develop new and better ways of producing the products and serving the customers. Too much prescription leads to bland uniformity and annihilates creativity.

💬 **Trust**

"Adding trust is the issue of the decade ... Without trust we cannot expect the human imagination to pursue value-added." (*The Tom Peters Seminar*)

FACILITATORS

One tool for developing a problem solving approach is the establishment of a core of skilled facilitators who are able to run creative problem solving sessions. There is obviously a cost involved in this development, but that can be more than offset by the effectiveness of this approach.

If you have taken on a personal commitment to organizing an army of liberation within your organization then this team of facilitators must be a wing of your army. Set up the team of facilitators

Group creativity

In a later chapter we'll look at how to facilitate a group creativity session. See p. 163.

from those already recruited to "the cause" or else convert experienced facilitators to creativity.

A word of warning. This is not an alternative to any of the other things that are being suggested in this section, or to developing individual creativity. Facilitators are a very effective way of encouraging the use of creativity for intractable problems, but they are quite ineffective at solving everyday problems which occur in the work place.

ROLE MODELS

The more individuals there are who do this stuff, the more the organization does this stuff. The more the individuals who do this stuff are seen as successful and rewarded for it, the more the rest of the organization will join in. It sounds easy, doesn't it? But you know it isn't. "Do as I say, not as I do" is endemic in corporate life. You should be making the effort to be otherwise. Make sure that the rebellious souls who form the core of the underground movement are successful. Find ways to encourage small, personal acts of rebellion. Demonstrate that you are willing to take part in large, public acts of rebellion.

INSTITUTIONAL SAFETY VALVES

Perhaps the best way to encourage creativity is to provide safety valves which legitimize criticism and challenge. The underground resistance movement is merely the organizing metaphor. There are individual safety valves which can fit in place in support of this movement. Our particular favorite is to employ a Corporate Jester. This is a job Paul invented for himself in British Airways. It does not involve walking around dressed in multicolored clothes with bells hanging from every appendage. It does involve using humor to challenge the stupidity which will inevitably happen from time to time in a large organization. It is a role which requires a willingness to put your head above the parapet. It is a role which will almost inevitably end in the incumbent being fired (or more probably, quietly hurried out of the back door in an unmarked vehicle). Above all it is a job

 Corporate Jesters
"His role is more serious than it sounds. BA has recognised that criticism softened by humor may be more effective than traditional forms of communication. Mr Birch tells top managers where they are going wrong and puts a smile on their faces at the same time."
(*The Guardian*, 12 October 1995)

which, for the right person, offers unrivalled opportunity to have a good time while improving the performance of the company.

TIMEOUT

Creativity blockers – practical dullness

It is almost a truism that in any idea generating session there will be someone who is assessing all of the ideas before they are fully formed. "But that's not practical!" is the cry. To which the creative response is, "So what?" Ideas do not need to be practical while they are being developed. In fact, a superb method of generating ideas is to find ideas which are not practical and to remove the obstacles to their practicality. There are people who make a rich living from finding expired patents which turned out to be impractical or poorly developed and then making them work. The fact that something is not or was not practical does not mean that it could not be made to be practical with a little work.

What is your organization's view of underground newspapers? Most organizations try to suppress them, the smarter ones try to control them. The really creative ones get hold of a copy, let them be and see where they lead. The criticism provided by a truly unfettered underground newspaper is an unmatched source of information about the things that are going wrong in a company.

Another useful safety valve is the provision of social clubs. This need not be anything grand, it could simply involve allowing staff the freedom to create and run them themselves. If they are too organized and too much part of the company they are merely an extension of the bureaucracy. Freeing them allows them to be an alternative.

Coming soon ➤ ➤ ➤

This has all seemed rather grim. The metaphor used has been very aggressive – the challenges of introducing creativity to an organization are formidable. But, allowing for the moments of pain that change always brings, using creativity can make your working life fun – and that's what's coming up after this message from our sponsors:

Key words

The underground resistance movement; assertive and arrogant (in a listening way); value difference; teams; risk taking; facilitators; role model; corporate jester.

126

BUSINESS AS USUAL (PART 1)

By Brian Clegg

"Why not? Tell me why not." Bernie Levin didn't really want to know. His tone said so. Bernie wanted results, not excuses. It was all there in his latest, best selling, management bible, "Levin Says Excellence Pays," which was sweeping corporate America as if they hadn't seen it three times before with different titles. "Don't accept that their excuse even exists", said his book, "and you'll get some action."

"I'll tell you what," said Levin, "let's pretend we were starting fresh. I'm a customer. I want to give you money – you know, the crinkly stuff that buys your meals – to fly me to Chicago. You're an airline. You're looking for customers to give you money to fly them to Chicago. It seems we have a terrific basis for a lasting relationship. And yet you are telling me I have to wait till Monday before I can fly. Can this be right?" It seemed it could be. Not only that, but there wasn't another airline prepared to do any better.

"This is incredible", Levin announced to his empty hotel suite when he had abandoned the phone. "Whoever decided airlines were in the service business needs a good session with a shrink." He pulled a leather bound notebook from an inner pocket and scrawled "Possible subject next book – Making Airlines Bearable" across the first vacant page. Two days. Two days in London with no-one to see, nothing to promote, and worst of all, nobody paying him for being there. It was unbelievable.

Levin took a beer from the mini-bar and slumped on the hotel's standard issue executive couch. It was the wrong shape for slouching. One by one he picked up the publications that the management had thoughtfully provided for his entertainment and flung them to the floor in an abstract display of uselessness.

"Welcome to your friendly hotel" – friendly, his ass. "The sights of London" – he'd seen it; his time was too precious to endure a repeat showing of the sights of London. "Country Life" – they had to be joking.

He held onto the last magazine, some sort of events guide, and flicked through it. Shows, he couldn't get excited about. They were too high risk an investment. Television wasn't for watching; he made television, he didn't watch it. All that remained were the small ads at the back, a jumbled mix of service lines and implausible descriptions of lonely people. If you believed half of what they'd written, they should be overwhelmed with admirers. They were losers, of course, each and every one. A splash of bold type at the bottom of the column caught his eye.

"Finding life dull? Thrive on adventure? Ring 0898-000000."

Nothing unusual there; it was likely to be a heavy breather line. There was no reason why it should interest him, yet it did. Telling himself he was going to regret it, he dialled.

When the ringing tone clicked off he thought he'd been proved right. There was the unmistakable sound of a well-used answering machine coming onto the line. But there was something about the voice, a female voice, that made him listen. There was nothing Bernie admired more in a woman than authority. You only had to look at his wife.

"Thank you for ringing Adventure Line. We aim to provide the ultimate relief from boredom. To begin the process, you need to be in the right frame of mind. Relax. Let your body go limp. Clear your thoughts of trouble … Now visualize your ultimate desire."

Levin laughed, not at the tape, but at himself for believing that it could be worthwhile. No doubt it would get onto the gynaecological details soon.

"I'm not the one with the dirty mind," said the tape. "Imagine the sort of adventure you want."

"What?" said Levin. "Who's there?"

"I'm waiting," said the tape. "Get visualizing."

"Don't mess me about. I want to speak to the manager."

"I'm waiting," said the tape again. "Have you no imagination?"

"This is ridiculous," thought Levin. "No answering machine is going to get the better of me. Hell, I invented creativity."

"That's better," said the tape, with excellent timing. "Next, picture your surroundings. Adventures have to start somewhere. See yourself about to set out on the experience of a lifetime."

"I've had the experience of a lifetime. It's called trying to get a seat on an airplane."

"You're rambling," said the tape. "Concentrate. Try to visualize."

Bernie visualized.

"And finally," said the tape, "finally comes payment. There can be no gain without pain. No benefit without investment."

"That's not bad," said Levin. "I could have written that."

"You will," said the tape. "For your final exercise, envision $2,000 in your bank account. See it, in your mind's eye, drifting out of the bank and into my hands." There was a pause. "Thank you for listening to Adventure Line," said the voice. "Enjoy." The line went dead.

Levin held the phone for a few, long seconds, then carefully put it back on the cradle. A deep laugh sent shock waves through his protuberant belly. They really had him going there for a moment. That was entertaining – someone in this pissant country had put together a neat little service. Perhaps he should find out more about Adventure Line; write it up as a case study for his next book.

A slithering noise disturbed his train of thought. Someone had pushed an envelope under the door. Despite his best efforts, life was determined to keep him from boredom. Levin rose from the deep couch and crossed the room. The envelope was sealed. Not cheap. It was not addressed, the only printing on it was a small logo in the top left hand corner: Adventure Line. Levin smiled to himself. Excellent. Not just originality, speed of service – definitely a case study. He ripped the envelope open.

Inside was a triple folded sheet of paper and something metallic, which dropped to the floor. Levin strained to reach over his stomach and pick the object up. It was a key, very like the key to his hotel room. He shrugged and returned to the couch, glancing through the letter as he went. He had to read it twice to believe it. Why ruin a superb service with a writing style that the worst time-share operator couldn't achieve? Re-reading didn't help. It was still the pits.

Congratulations, Mr Levin!

*Thanks to Adventure Line, you, **Mr Levin**, have won the adventure of your dreams.*

*This opportunity is not available to anyone. We could have picked any single floor in the **Regency Hotel**. Lady Luck was smiling on your floor, **Mr Levin**, the **twenty-third** floor. But there were still thirty-seven rooms in the running. Thirty-seven rooms with a once-in-a-lifetime chance. We narrowed it down still further, carefully sifting, selecting the ideal room to be a winner. And that room was yours, **Mr Levin**. Room 2306.*

*You are already a winner. There is no further draw; there's just one thing to do. Take the personalized key enclosed in this envelope. Take it straight away and use it to open the door of room 2319. Walk straight in to receive your prize. And do it now, **Mr Levin**. Time is of the essence if you are to become an Adventure Line winner. I know you won't be disappointed.*

Yours adventurously,

Indecipherable squiggle

President and Chief Executive of the Adventure Line Corporation

Levin put the offending sheet down beside him and twisted the key between his fingers. Should he try it? It could be a set up, a plot to dirty his name. It wasn't easy to stay on top as a management guru. You had to hustle. But he was a big boy. He'd got out of that blackmail attempt in '88 with a $100,000 out-of-court settlement – in his favor. Levin gripped the key firmly in his hand and set out for room 2319.

It wasn't far. Levin looked up and down the corridor, fighting off a combination of guilt and prurience. What was on offer in this room? What could provide the adventure of his dreams? He suppressed a mental image of his wife; there was no sound, but her very posture said "don't do it." The key

 Belief systems
Either those responsible for this kind of letter are suffering from a delusion that the public is very stupid, or they are playing a game, along the lines of "we know it's stupid and they know it's stupid, but it's traditional."

was hard and cold in his hand. He slipped it into the lock. The door opened on absolute darkness, a blank void that the dim corridor lights could not penetrate. Reluctantly, Levin slipped his head into the room. It was so dark that he expected his face to be buffeted by a sheet of black velvet, but there was only air.

Levin relaxed, breathing for the first time in many seconds. He felt along the wall beside the doorway, hunting for the light switch. It wasn't there. His fingers met nothing more than the faint, grainy texture of the wallpaper.

Levin whispered to himself: "Where is the goddamn thing?" He took a step forward to reach further along the wall. The carpet seemed strangely fluid, reluctant to support his weight. It was as if he was walking on a water bed.

Levin glanced back at the door. A cold vice of fear gripped his throat. The door had gone. No, that wasn't true, the door was in the process of becoming gone. It was receding as if he was falling, or it was falling, or even both of them were falling, only in two different directions, neither of them down. He watched the rectangle fade to a dot before nothingness was everywhere.

Everywhere but underneath him. Before he had time to be scared, a strong pressure lifted his knees, leaving him in a seated position. A bubble of light swelled from beneath to encompass him entirely. Without noticing any transition, he was sitting in a huge leather chair behind an imposing desk. A desk that bore only three things. A blotter, almost as good as the one on his own desk. A photograph of a man and a woman, his own photograph, the one he always carried. And a prism-shaped piece of polished wood, presumably a name plate.

Levin hesitated before reaching out for the plate. He thought he knew who he was, but events were moving too fast. Given his experience to date it would be unwise for him to assume anything. But, hell, what was he scared of? He twisted the plate around with a spasmodic jerk of his arm.

BERNIE LEVIN – CHIEF EXECUTIVE OFFICER, GENERAL ELECTRONICS

Bernie's eyebrows tried to follow his receding hairline on an exploratory trip up his forehead. The whites of his eyes were showing clearly as they scanned the elegantly furnished room and returned to the seemingly empty desktop. Seemingly, because a moment later a phone rang. Somewhere. A squawk box squawked. Fax paper issued smoothly from a narrow orifice. A computer screen popped up from under the blotter. Suddenly life was very busy.

For the moment, let's leave Bernie to it. Somewhere else, somewhere so remarkably else that it is quite impossible to specify without using five dimensional tensors, some very satisfying cursing and screaming was going on. The center of the storm was Liane Schwartz, newly promoted Comptroller of Adventure Line. To say that Liane was unhappy would be like describing a dog whose favorite bone has just been turned into fertilizer as mildly miffed. This was serious pique.

"Is being a traffic jam a way of life with you, or just a hobby?" she asked a creature who had the audacity to come between her and her goal. A creature which it would be easy to mistake for a twelve foot high, albino, hairless gorilla. Easy isn't the word; it was a push over. After all, it was a twelve foot high, albino, hairless gorilla.

"That's a tough one, init," said the gorilla. "It's like a subjective judgement, know what I mean? On the one hand you've got your way of life, your very core of being. Something you couldn't change if you wanted to. On the other hand there's your hobby, your archetypal spare time activity. But where does the interface between them come? Where indeed, for we speak of a paper-fine distinction of cobweb fragility and frightening complexity." The gorilla spoiled the subtlety of its argument by excavating one of its nostrils with a long, hairless finger.

"I don't believe my ears!" exploded Liane. "Here's me with the greatest crisis of my career and I'm faced with a philosophical monkey. Make that a bald, philosophical monkey. Now are you going to move or am I going to have to make you?"

It said something for the sheer force of Liane's personality that the ape moved without so much as a murmur. Just how much it said can only be fully appreciated when it is realized that Liane was only three inches high. To the gorilla she was little more than a bright red, animated blob. A very small blob.

Liane stomped down the corridor, scattering the manifold employees of Adventure Line who had, until that moment, thought it a perfectly marvellous afternoon for a stroll through the office complex. Now they knew different. Ahead was one of the control rooms, the nerve centers where dedicated employees monitored the delicate progress of their product, easing up the sense of danger here, adding a touch of romance there. Each nuance of the experience could be subtly adjusted, using complex panels that made the average sound mixer look like something from Toys R Us. Liane hurled herself through the smallest of the three doors and activated the lift that ran up to the shelf above.

She stamped across the surface of the control desk, a huge, glaciated plain viewed from her minuscule scale, and planted herself firmly in front of the duty supervisor. There was something suspiciously theatrical about the way she posed with one miniature foot, clad in an inch-long, gleaming black leather boot, on the slider in front of her. The supervisor regarded his boss's boss with a calmness that many would regard as a hybrid of stupidity and innocence. His long, floppy ears, which contrasted oddly with his otherwise

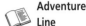
Adventure Line

And Liane Schwartz features in an unpublished full-length novel (working title *Figments*) by Brian Clegg. Watch the shelves.

humanoid appearance and his impeccable double-breasted suit, lay back over his shoulders, giving him an air of relaxed ease that approached unconsciousness.

"You are handling the Levin case," said Liane. She made it sound like an accusation of murder. Particularly unpleasant murder.

"Sure thing," said the supervisor. His name, which has no relevance to the plot but is added to include a hint of local color, was Ridley Overlay. He smiled the sort of goofy smile usually the sole property of the insane and besotted teenagers. He was neither.

"You didn't perhaps think there was anything noteworthy about the case? Something to flag up with your manager? Perhaps even something I should be alerted to?"

"Well …" said Overlay, a closet James Stewart fan, "No." He scratched himself behind the right ear. This would not have been noteworthy had he not used his left foot.

"Smooth talker, aren't you? We have a major complaint situation here. I'm going to have to handle this myself, bunny ears. Get my drift? If I get hassle, you're looking for somewhere else to hang up your carrot. Capisce?"

Despite a laid-backness that tended to the horizontal, Overlay had a mortgage to pay. "Understood, sir," he said. "What do you want me to do with Levin?"

"Mr Levin. Politeness at all times, screw-head. Have him sent to the interview room on level two. Make sure he's well and truly relaxed by the time I get there." Liane seemed to notice there was a hint of a frown on the supervisor's brow. "Is there a problem, mister?"

"No, certainly not. No problem at all, you just leave it to me."

"Of course. I believe in delegation." Liane headed for the lift. She turned on the threshold, waiting until the doors were starting to close. "Oh, and Overlay, I also believe in capital punishment." The doors smacked shut with a satisfying thunk.

… to be continued

MAKING WORK FUN

Work = fun

A great book which explores this area more fully and with a wonderfully humorous touch is David Firth, *How To Make Work Fun!* (Gower, 1995).

Have you ever talked to anyone who really enjoys their job? Not someone who likes it better than the alternatives available right now. Not someone who enjoys it because of the way they can spend the money earned. Someone who gets so much fun from their work that they can't help buttonholing you and telling you what fun it is. There are not many of us around.

When you find someone like this, grab hold of them. Hang on to them. Analyse them. Find out what it is about them and their job that makes them this way. They are valuable. Anyone who really enjoys their work is a very precious commodity. They will be adding value to their business in ways you couldn't even imagine, in places you can't even see. They will be hunting for ways to make things better for themselves, their colleagues and the business. Most importantly, and the reason for having this chapter in the book, they will be increasing the level of creativity in their organization by a significant degree. We believe that there is a direct relationship between fun and creativity. It isn't something we can prove with mountains of academic studies but it is demonstrable that creative organizations are also fun organizations.

A master at work

For a classic case of someone who found work fun (and was stunningly creative), read Richard P. Feynman, *Surely you're joking, Mr Feynman!* (Vintage, 1985) – hilarious remembrances from the Nobel prize winning physicist.

There will be many similarities between this chapter and the one on institutionalizing creativity. This is hardly surprising since a fun environment is more likely to be a creative environment. Let us hope that this does not seem repetitious. Whilst repetition can help learning it can be dull. Repetition can help learning but can be dull. What we mean is that repeating what you say can be boring despite its obvious aid to learning.

LOOK AFTER OTHERS

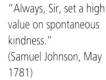

Kindness

"Always, Sir, set a high value on spontaneous kindness." (Samuel Johnson, May 1781)

Do yourself a favor by doing someone else a favor. Try doing a couple of acts of kindness, not with a view to what you'll get out of it but because it is quite a fun thing to do. Not only that, the people you consider in this way think that it's quite positive. The effect of this adds up – before you know it there are many small acts of kindness being done by a whole bunch of people all over the place. The best bit of all is that everyone is enjoying this and the atmosphere improves significantly as a result.

Doing favors can be personal or it can be business related. We often develop attitudes in business which mean that doing our job in support of our department is more important than helping the company to achieve better results. No-one is going to say this explicitly, of course, but watch the way people around you behave. Starting a habit of helping out others, of doing favors which are in support of others and working to the greater good of the company improves the feel good factor but also directly improves other people's ability to do their job.

LITTLE THINGS MEAN A LOT

The small things in your life and the lives of others can have more impact on your enjoyment than the big things. We remember the momentous events but we also treasure the small acts of kindness we have experienced. It is also far easier to arrange a series of small events than one large one. Next time one of the people you work with puts in a special effort, give them a small token as a thank you. When you next return home why not take a present for your partner – a bunch of flowers or a box of chocolates. For those of you thinking that the assumption here is that your partner is a woman, that is not the case. A few months ago Paul did some work with the London International Festival of Theatre and as a thank you they presented him with a bunch of flowers. Taking it home on the tube was great fun. Everyone he met assumed that he had bought it for his wife. Explaining that it was his was part of the enjoyment but getting it in the first place was just wonderful.

What can you buy?

Make a list now of the small gifts you could get for people as a thank you. It should be relatively easy to think of the likes and dislikes of your partner but what about the people you work with? How well do you know them?

TIMEOUT

Creativity blockers – being serious

Business is about making money. Making money is serious business. This book is aimed at increasing business creativity so it must be serious. The techniques it teaches must be serious. The application of those techniques must be serious. Wrong! Yes, it is important to take some aspects of business seriously. Most business people have heavy responsibilities. It would be outrageous of them to ignore these.

In many cases it would also be illegal. This does not mean that any and every aspect of business life must be serious. We believe passionately that business should be fun. We also believe that fun businesses can be more successful. Creative ideas flow from not being serious. Be frivolous, even play around. Take business seriously by all means. Take creativity seriously if you must but please, don't take yourself seriously.

Resumé and Rolodex

Tom Peters suggests that you should manage your career through your resumé and Rolodex (c.v. and contact list). Every three months re-write your c.v. and add anything you have done which you think is significant. Also check that you are continually adding new contacts. Aim for more outside your organization than inside.

What did you learn today?

Take a few minutes now to list the things you have learned so far today. If that list is short then add those things you have learned in the last week. Think about the life of a small child. Every minute of every day is packed with learning. You do not know so much about the world that you couldn't benefit from this level of learning.

NETWORKING – WHAT AN AWFUL WORD!

But what a great idea! It isn't about maintaining contacts because they might be useful to you one day (even though they might). It's about maintaining contacts because you want to; because you like them. Those who maintain a contact list on this basis will enjoy the contacts more and probably get more out of the relationships than those who have a purely instrumental view of networking. Enter relationships wondering what you can do to benefit the other party, not the other way round. The things you do will usually cost you little, they will always be well remembered and will probably be repaid in the future. What goes around, comes around.

LEARN SOMETHING NEW EVERY DAY

This cannot be stressed enough. At the heart of enjoying work, life and everything else, is the sense of wonder at the world that you had as a child. Taking things apart to see how they work may not be practical when those things are organizations or other people but this is no excuse for not being curious about their working. In an opinion column in *PC Pro* magazine, journalist Dick Pountain bemoaned the way "sad" has come to mean uncool, because you are interested in things. "The current concept of sadness is just another way of saying that consumption is cooler than production," says Pountain. If that's the case, like Pountain we urge you to be glad to be sad. Learning is a great spur to enjoyment – why lead a dull life, without curiosity and joy, just to conform?

Do you know any really creative individuals – people who are generally identified as the ones always sparking new ideas and off-the-wall suggestions? Talk with them about learning. I am willing to bet that they have an open attitude to any new input. They will probably be very aware of current affairs. They will certainly read a great deal of both fiction and non-fiction. They will have a wide range of interests and will be actively involved in developing these. Emulate them.

WHAT IS IMPORTANT TO YOU?

You cannot easily set about increasing the level of fun in a systematic way unless you know what matters to you. Okay, you may be thinking, of course I know what's important; how does that help? Do you really know what is important to you? Do you really? One of us heard Ken Blanchard a few years ago talking about a good friend of his who was a rabbi who said that he had been at many deathbeds and had never heard anyone say, "My God, I wish I had spent more time at the office." What will you be saying on your deathbed? What will be your regrets?

Alternatively, try the lottery test. If you came up on a major lottery tomorrow and were suddenly a multi-millionaire, if you never had to do another day's work in order to satisfy your needs, which of the activities you currently undertake would you still do? What would you start doing that you currently don't? Once you have clarified what is important this way, make sure that you reflect the importance in the time and effort you put into these areas. It's crucial to make work fun.

What is important?
Use your right brain to find out. Take a pile of color magazines and catalogues and tear out any pictures which appeal to you. When you have hundreds of them start to stick them onto a large sheet of paper as a collage. Study that collage for a while and use it as a spur to help you understand the things that appeal and the things that are important.

 **TIMEOUT**

Kekulé

The German chemist Friedrich August Kekulé von Stradonitz is best known for formulating the theory of the ring structure of benzene in 1865 from the patterns in a coal fire.

In his own words, "I turned my chair to the fire and dozed. Again the atoms were gambolling before my eyes. This time the smaller groups kept modestly in the background. My mental eye, rendered more acute by repeated visions of this kind, could now distinguish larger structures, in manifold confirmation; long rows sometimes more closely fitted together, all turning and twisting in snake-like motion. But look! What was that? One of the snakes had seized hold of its own tail and the form whirled mockingly before my eyes. As if by a flash of lightning I awoke."

The results of Kekulé's investigations into the linking of carbon atoms in organic compounds were vital to the development of organic chemistry. Through his dozing he was able to introduce the concept of tetravalent carbon atoms joined to each other and to other atoms in the molecules of organic compounds.

SMILE!

Now for the hardest piece of advice of all. Stand in front of a mirror and look at your face. Try making a variety of movements with the muscles of the face. You may well notice that every so often the corners of your mouth turn up. Hold that. Now look at your eyes. Sometimes the edges crinkle and a sparkle comes to them. Work on combining these movements; especially when you feel good.

This is called a smile. You used to do this quite a lot as a child and have probably got out of the habit. Don't worry, it will come back to you with a little practice. Before long you will even find yourself smiling at work. This is not a dismissal offense. You will not get fired for smiling or for obviously enjoying what you do. You may get odd looks but you will not get fired. Try it. It is a great feeling when it gets to be habitual. For the advanced students there is another exercise called laughter. This is even better for you and even more fun – but for most of you it might be too soon for that.

WHY NOT START TODAY?

This is the sort of text that you either read and dismiss or read and say, "Yes, I must do that some time." It is rare that you read this sort of thing and do something about it. Change the habits of a lifetime. Start now. Use earlier examples and suggestions as a provocation to action here.

Coming soon ➤➤➤

Everything we've mentioned so far can be achieved with a pencil, a piece of paper and a brain (ideally not detached). But the computer can provide an excellent support mechanism for creativity.

Key thoughts

- Don't wear tight underpants (relax a little)
- Smile, laugh and enjoy life – you'll be sorry later if you don't
- Be glad to be sad.

BUSINESS AS USUAL (PART 2)

By Brian Clegg

It was almost a disappointment to Liane Schwartz, the Comptroller of Adventure Line, that when she reached Levin, he seemed to be enjoying a bowl of coffee. Liane liked to get the best out of disaster, to milk it for all it was worth. She would have to find somebody else to shout at. Levin looked up as the sliding doors opened. Looked up, around, and only with a growing realization that the world continued to be unpredictable, finally looked down.

"What's the matter?" said Liane. "Didn't your mother teach you that it's rude to stare at anyone, let alone a lady."

"I'm sorry," said Levin, looking quickly to the ceiling. "I've never seen such a small …" He realized that there was something wrong here. He was the complainant. He was the one who should be receiving the apologies. "Are you the manager? I have a complaint."

"I am the Comptroller of Adventure Line." Liane advanced up a sloping ramp that brought her onto the coffee table in the middle of the room.

Levin squinted to see her better. His optician had been trying to get him into a stronger prescription for years. "So?" he said, deciding that he wasn't going to let a matter of size – or Liane's carved-ice beauty – get in the way of his sense of disgruntlement. "What's that, some sort of secretary?"

"The Comptroller has total day-to-day responsibility for the Adventure Line operations, Mr Levin. In the words of one of your presidents, the dough stops here."

"That's buck, not doe."

"Buck, dough – it's all money, isn't it? As is my time, Mr Levin. I believe you have a complaint."

"I certainly do. Your service is supposed to fulfill my desires, isn't it? Let's forget the way I was precipitously dumped into this so-called adventure – it doesn't make my day, but I can live with it. What I can't comprehend is why you should think that running a major corporation is my idea of a dream. I never wanted that."

"Just a moment, Mr Levin, let me, er …" Liane thumbed through a tiny folder. "It's here somewhere. Okay. Didn't you write in your last book but one, 'Success is about change; if you don't find the prospect of taking the reins of a large company and turning it around the most thrilling thing since being born, you haven't got the initiative to blow your own nose.' Wasn't that you, Mr Levin? Could it have been some other Bernie V. Levin?"

"I may have written that," said Levin, flustered. "I write a lot of things. But that doesn't …"

"How about this, Mr Levin? 'By employing my simple creative management checklist, you may not double your profits overnight, but you'll have a damned good try. That's what I call real fulfillment.' Wasn't that from 'The Creative Manager'?"

"I think it may be," said Levin, "but you miss my point. I'm a consultant. I write books about how to run companies; I make videos about how to run companies; hell, I even make tee-shirts about how to run companies. I go in and advise. I lecture. I recommend. But *I* do not actually run the things. That's no turn-on for me."

"It isn't?" For the first time, Liane showed a hint of uncertainty. "You really don't want to run a company; it's not your secret dream?"

"Do you think I couldn't buy a company if I wanted one? I make enough money by telling other people what to do to buy a string of companies. You're going to have to do better than that, lady."

"I must apologise," said Liane. "Our research department is usually very thorough." She picked up something that Levin had assumed was a purple paper clip and muttered into it. There seemed to be no reply. "I'm sorry about this," said Liane, "the phones are down again. Getting any action out of the maintenance department is impossible. Stay there a moment, would you?"

She walked calmly down the ramp, over to the sliding doors and bellowed at a passing dwarf in an unbelievably powerful voice for one so small: "Hey, you!"

"Me?" said the dwarf, skidding to an unscheduled stop.

"Got it in one, shortarse."

Luckily for the dwarf's career she suppressed the obvious reply. "I am on a job right now, Comptroller."

"Well deduced," said Liane. "Specifically you are going to extract Mr Levin's account from the files and bring it here immediately. That's the job you're on."

"Thank you, Comptroller."

"You're welcome," said Liane. "Be back in under five minutes if you want to keep that beard."

The dwarf paled noticeably beneath the fashionable dirt that she had smeared onto her cheeks. The effect was supposed to reflect the continuity of modern dwarfdom with their mining heritage. In fact it looked more like she'd accidentally mopped her face with an oily rag. Such is the disadvantage of being a slave to fashion. And no fashion was more essential to a dwarf than her (or his) beard. As usual, Liane's threat had hit the nail on the head so hard that it had been bent double.

"We'll have this sorted out in a moment," said Liane. She was putting a lot of effort into smiling sweetly, which was completely wasted on Levin who had difficulty even picking out her mouth.

"Your accounts are filed manually?" said Levin.

"Don't talk to me about accounts," said Liane. She sat on a small grey object that Levin had assumed was an abandoned sugar lump and crossed her legs. The full length of her boots glinted in the light from the nearby desk lamp. Levin squinted hard. "The place is in chaos. I really ought not to be telling a customer this, but I feel I can trust you." She moved one leg against the other in a way that Levin found ridiculously stimulating. After all, how could he be attracted by someone three inches high? It was hardly practical.

"Could I see that?"

"I'm sorry?" said Liane. "See what?"

"Your accounts department. I'd like to see your accounts department."

"I don't see why not," said Liane. "It's hardly regular, but we have messed you about. Come this way."

Levin hauled himself out of the chair and took a single step. Already he was in front of Liane. He waited for the tiny woman to get out into the corridor, taking single paces interspersed with long pauses to let her get ahead again.

"This is it," said Liane, stopping by a high pair of doors. Levin stepped into the room beyond, holding the door for Liane. Room was perhaps the wrong word. It was more like a Victorian engineer's attempt at designing a 747 aircraft hangar. A highly eccentric Victorian engineer. The vast space was criss-crossed with a tangle of girders and shelves and ramps and pneumatic tubes and racks and very strange people.

"What's going on?" said Levin in a whisper.

"The account form comes in there," said Liane pointing into the far distance. "It then goes into a small, dark cupboard in the far corner, usually for a couple of weeks."

"A couple of weeks? Why, for heaven's sake?"

"We need several copies of the form," said Liane. "They only breed when they've been left in warm, dark cupboards for a couple of weeks."

"Breed?"

"You know. Multiply. Have babies. It must happen in your world."

"Never mind," said Levin, "take that as read. What happens next?"

"They go all over the place. Hang on." Liane put two tiny fingers into her mouth and whistled a devastating blast. A large figure detached itself from sorting papers on a nearby table. As it got closer, Levin realized that it hadn't been nearby at all. It had a long way to come. Further than he could have imagined. And that meant it was more than large. It was huge. Vaguely man-shaped, it towered over him, like an American football quarterback over a ball.

"Wha ... wha ..." Bernie seemed to be having trouble with his word formation.

"This is Geld," said Liane.

"Shall I hit him now, miss?" asked the immense creature. Some emotional response creased the vast slit mouth in its grey-white face.

"You're not to hit him, Geld," said Liane. "Geld's a mountain troll, Mr Levin. It has a wide ranging role in accounts."

"That's nice," said Bernie. There wasn't much else to say, faced with Geld.

"I could tread on him a bit," said Geld. "He looks squishy to me." Now he was definitely smiling. "I like treading on people and the squishy ones are the best. You don't have to pick fragments of carapace out from between your toes with the squishy ones."

"No, Geld," said Liane. "Mr Levin is not a debt collection case. He doesn't owe us any money. He wants to see how the accounts department works. Could you take him through it?"

"If you say so, miss," said the troll. "Couldn't I just bite one of his arms off? It wouldn't amount to much, but it would give me a great deal of simple pleasure."

"No," said Liane. "I'm sorry, Mr Levin; duty calls, but I'm sure you will be very comfortable in Geld's capable hands."

"Now look …" said Bernie. He didn't have a chance to say anything more before the troll took Liane literally. Very soon Bernie was going to discover that travelling in a troll's pocket was not a pleasant experience.

"… a 25 percent increase in throughput without any extra manpower overhead. That about wraps up my presentation."

"Thank you very much, Mr Levin." Liane sat further back in her chair. "I will be considering all your suggestions, and I'm sure we'll be able to transform our operation, thanks to your efforts."

"You're very kind," said Bernie. He had entirely forgotten his original intention of complaint, and the way Liane had dumped him with that mobile mountain. In the space of a couple of days he had penetrated to the depths of their creaking, uncompetitive organization and had put together a report that was so precise, so elegant, it wouldn't look out of place in an art gallery. He was happy, filled with a post-consultal glow. "There's just the matter of fees."

"It's quite standard," said Liane. "There's a flat rate. You heard our terms when you telephoned. I believe you accepted them at the time."

"Hang on there, young lady, I mean my fees. You have just had the services of the best in the business. I don't come cheap."

"Oh dear," said Liane. She shook her head vigorously. "Oh dear, no. I don't think you understand the nature of the transaction. You pay us, we deliver the adventure. That's the only point money changes hands, I assure you. We never pay our customers."

Key thoughts

- The problem is often not the obvious one
- A good solution is tailored to the individual
- Work that's fun sometimes catches you by surprise.

"But it went wrong." Levin's forehead was developing a worrying purple hue. "My adventure was a catastrophe. I have never seen a business more in need of help. I thought the sort of organizational practices you've got went out with the Byzantine Empire. I mean, I've seen better organized tax offices. I've worked my ass off straightening out your procedures. Your service did not deliver. It all went wrong."

"Did it?" said Liane. Her smile was so broad that even Bernie could pick it out. "Did it really?"

COMPUTER-SUPPORTED CREATIVITY

■ **Can computers be creative?**

■ **Another tool**

■ **Using conventional office software**

■ **Products to stimulate creativity**

■ **Creativity on-line**

Creativity with a LAN / Innovative Internet / Feeling blank? /
So how do I get it?

Creative machines
Science fiction has numerous examples of computers and robots which are creative or self-aware. See, for example, Isaac Asimov, *I Robot*, Robert Heinlein, *The Moon is a Harsh Mistress*, John Sladek, *Roderick*. For an attempt at realism, try Harry Harrison & Marvin Minsky, *The Turing Option*.

CAN COMPUTERS BE CREATIVE?

There's something very uncomfortable about the image of machines being creative. Not only is it offensive to the view which sees creativity as a principal part of our humanity, it is threatening. We have become used to being bettered by machines in the physical world – in strength, in speed – and to their superiority at mechanical mental tasks such as arithmetic. But there was always the comfortable assurance that we retained the jewel of creativity. Machines could not create, only reproduce.

In extolling computer-supported creativity, we are (for once) not threatening all that you hold dear. Although it's arguable that some human "creativity" could easily be performed by computer (producing a formula best-seller, perhaps), there is still a huge gulf between what the computer can manage by combining a library of information with rules and randomness, and the creativity of even the most mundane human – at least, with the aid of this book.

But we still think that computers are one of the best things to have happened in the pursuit of creativity, and they should not be viewed as an opponent or a threat, but just as another tool like the pen or phone.

ANOTHER TOOL

Once the computer is reduced to the position of a tool, how can it help? In exactly the same way as the rest of our toolkit, the computer is capable of being a mechanical stimulus to help us break out of a conventional mode of thought.

What's more, the personal computer (PC) is an ideal vehicle to support many of the techniques we recommend. Generating random numbers to pick a word from a large bank of options is a trivial task for a computer. Some techniques fit less well. Although there are some effective tools for generating mind maps on PCs, it is difficult to be as quick and free as you can when sketching out on a large sheet of paper. The ideal is a mix of computer tools and pen-and-paper work.

TIMEOUT

Creativity blockers – avoiding mistakes

I want you to be very careful. Don't make a slip. Mistakes are, as everybody knows, bad things. We learn techniques for avoiding them. We check our work. If we are careful individuals we double or even triple check. This habit extends from things we produce to ideas we are producing. We check our ideas. If we are careful individuals we double or even triple check them. By the time we have finished this process we have collected a long list of things that are wrong with the idea. They tie themselves around its legs and drag it to the bottom of the ocean. It will never surface again. The things about the idea which were good are dragged down with it. They will never be seen again either.

If, in developing ideas, we had allowed ourselves mistakes, then we could have held onto the good items and progressively removed the bad points as they appeared. We might even have found that some of the bad points turned out to be the real benefits of the idea. If only we had allowed ourselves to make mistakes. Well, we live and learn.

USING CONVENTIONAL OFFICE SOFTWARE

Even if you don't intend to buy software specifically written to aid creativity, if you've got a PC, the chances are that you will have something you can use. Take a word processor – the one we've used to put this book together (Microsoft Word) has two key features for creative work. There's an outliner, which is an excellent cheap and cheerful way of structuring thoughts – you could use it for doing an aerial survey, making the top heading levels the branches of your map, the next level the twigs from the branches and so on.

There's also a spell checker and thesaurus. Try the spell checker as a way of generating random words. Type some gobbledegook that looks like a word but isn't: we tried "rudsot." The spell checker changed it to "rudest." From there we could start generating ideas. You need a bit of patience with this technique as it will often say "no suggestions." A good way to try to avoid forming a word intentionally is to alter one letter at a time from random typing until the spell checker finds an answer. We originally used pudsot in the above example.

Splot
The children's word processor Creative Writer has an idea generator called the Splot Machine, but this is too limited for true creativity.

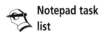

Notepad task list

Using a notepad program or word processor, put together a prioritized task list for the upcoming weekend. Notice how the ability to insert at any point makes this easy.

E-mail

Electronic mail via linked computers. These e-mail addresses will reach us from any of the on-line services discussed below.

Brian Clegg:
brian@cul.co.uk

Paul Birch:
Paul_S_Birch@msn.com

The thesaurus is handy for generating an alternative word as a variant of the level chain. Say you were looking for a new way of packaging CDs. You might start with jewel case (the name given to the current CD box). Word's thesaurus comes up with brooch, badge, jewellery, and pin for jewel, while case produces a whole raft of possibilities including box, sheet, and chest. Already some ideas spring to mind. CDs are often very attractive – perhaps they should be sold in a container which would enable them to be pinned to your chest? Maybe not, but it's a start.

Even a simple notepad program has a huge advantage over a piece of paper as you can structure information as you enter it. Try using a CD encyclopedia as stimulation, too. Type random letters into the search and use the result like a random picture.

PRODUCTS TO STIMULATE CREATIVITY

If you need more than a general purpose program can provide, there are a number of commercial products to help with creativity.

The most interesting ones fit into two categories. Some are idea mapping products, which enable the computer to be used to generate mind maps and similar structured diagrams. Products on the market include Inspiration, VisiMap, Mind Manager and Corkboard. We've used a number of these, but often fall back to paper and pens. Quick entry packages like VisiMap are good for capturing ideas on the fly, while products like Mind Manager produce elegant diagrams – but you can't beat the flexibility of the pen.

The second set are programs which seek actively to stimulate ideas. These vary from an electronic version of Roger von Oech's Creative Whack Pack, through list based stimulation from MindLink and Idea-Fisher, to probably the most complex support from the Axon Idea Processor.

We have developed a piece of shareware that supports the Imagination Engineering framework, plus some free software for idea generation. For more information on these and the packages above see the Creativity Unleashed web site http://www.cul.co.uk

Float glass

Making glass perfectly smooth and clear has always been a problem. This was to some extent overcome by the plate glass process which involves rolling the glass on a flat surface or between two parallel rollers. This process requires costly grinding and polishing once the glass is made.

Pondering this problem while washing up one evening, Alastair Pilkington, of Pilkington glass, watched a bar of soap floating in the water. He visualized glass floating and realized that this would be a way to produce a high quality surface.

As a direct result of the floating soap bar he developed the float-glass process. In this process clear, flat surfaces are formed on both sides by floating a sheet of glass on top of a bath of molten tin. The high temperature is gradually lowered as the glass moves along the tin bath, and the glass passes through a long annealing oven at the end. The resulting high quality glass is manufactured more cheaply than the rolling process can manage.

 TIMEOUT

 Floating soap
The only problem with this story is that soap doesn't float. It's possible, of course, that Mr Pilkington had a plastic duck in his bath and that was what he observed, but didn't want to admit it. Alternatively it might have been a film of soap on the surface. Whatever he observed, the effect was the same.

CREATIVITY ON-LINE

There was a time when the packages you purchased off the shelf would form the limit of any discussion of creativity as delivered by computers. Now the introduction of local area networks (LANs) to the business environment and the ubiquitous nature of the Internet (it no longer seems strange when a children's television program gives an Internet address for contact with its viewers) bring new opportunities to put the muscle of the electronic world behind your problem solving and idea generation.

 LAN
Local area network. Common means of linking PCs to enable rapid information sharing and collaboration.

Scanners

These devices to get photographs and documents into a PC are much less widely available in business than other peripherals. This might be because they are regarded as frivolous, but they are often useful in computer supported creativity.

Level chain technique

See p. 32.

10 minutes

Give an electronic level chain a try. Write an e-mail describing the level chain method, then choose around ten correspondents you know well. Send the e-mail to the first with instructions to add one link and send it onto the next. Use it on an idea you want help with, or test out the principle by starting from the paper clip and looking for a new piece of office hardware. If you don't have e-mail, you could always do it via fax or the post, but it will be slower.

■ Creativity with a LAN

It's getting to the stage that it's unusual not to have local area networking in any business worth its salt. This is the technology by which individual personal computers are connected up to enable the sharing of information and services through a high-speed link which does not involve making a telephone call. The LAN is a very powerful tool, which is often underutilized. Here's a chance to get more out of it and the tools which reside on it.

Pretty well any LAN setup will enable the sharing of disk files. How about a virtual brainstorm? Put a document on a shared drive containing a brief survey of the problem (a small mind map might be useful if you can scan one in) and invite contributions. Let it be widely known that you are looking for thoughts – perhaps put some restrictions in place, or use a random word technique to stimulate ideas from the contributors.

If you have electronic mail software, you can take this approach one stage further. How about an electronic level chain? Put together an e-mail with a brief description of the level chain technique (if your e-mail supports attachments, it would be best to attach this separately). Put in a seed idea and a description of what you are trying to achieve. Then send the mail to someone you know. Ask them to add one link to the chain and forward the mail to someone else. Each correspondent can start a new chain or add to the current one. Ask the recipient on a certain date – perhaps a week after starting the process – to send the mail back to you.

If you are feeling really brave, you can send out perhaps a dozen originals to different recipients. There are, however, a couple of dangers of using a widespread electronic chain message. One is incurring the wrath of the IT people responsible for your e-mail network. As a creative person, you have to be prepared to upset bureaucracy now and again – this is a case where you need to face up to them and ask if your use of the e-mail system to solve a key business problem (which is what you ought to be using it for) is somehow less important than the miles of trivia which generally wings its way from user to user. Point out that this might be one of the rare occasions when it would be possible to make a business case for the existence of e-mail (and possibly even the people who support it).

The more significant danger is irritating the people you send the mail to. Receiving such a request once every few months can be quite entertaining. Receiving one a week will quickly become an irritation. Make sure that this technique is used infrequently and with discretion.

E-mail is an active communication mechanism, the electronic equivalent of sending a letter through the post, which arrives on your doorstep, prompting you to open and read it (or in the case of junk mail, bin it unread). But e-mail has a passive relation – the electronic bulletin board. Whether in the basic form present in most e-mail or at the level of sophistication of groupware products like Lotus Notes, the bulletin board is a means to place a document or information in an available space, which then can be looked at by those who are interested, but does not have the intrusive nature of e-mail.

While e-mail chains are the best way to get a quick response without a well-established grouping, posting a problem for group discussion on a bulletin board is less obtrusive and can be used with a frequency which would cause a degree of resentment in an e-mail form. Such approaches can be subject oriented – having a bulletin board area dedicated to the particular subject – or general. The latter is more likely to be fruitful, as the best ideas often come from those who do not normally think of themselves as involved in the problem area. Why not talk to your IT people about having an ideas bulletin board which anyone interested can look at, and contribute to solutions for the various problems which are facing the business.

Don't limit yourself to simply asking for ideas, make use of the Imagination Engineering structure and techniques to stimulate your contributors into being more creative. With modern software, almost all of the techniques we describe (scanning a photograph for the random picture technique, for example) could be used.

The biggest danger with the bulletin board approach is the anorak effect. It seems that, while many will browse and occasionally contribute to bulletin boards, there will often be a hard core of contributors who make the vast majority of the entries. Such people are often stuck in a certain track, and so tend not to offer particularly creative input. Whatever you do, don't try to ban these people. Not only can they be extremely disruptive, but proper involvement might

Groupware
Any software which helps a group of people work together better could be described as groupware, but it ideally should support the business processes which make the group more than a collection of individuals.

Anorak
This harmless garment has become a term of mild abuse in the UK, due to its popularity with railway enthusiasts. A suspicion of the interest of grown adults in such a harmless pursuit has led to media pillorying for train spotters, and hence the use of the garment as a term for a technical enthusiast who needs to get a life.

bring them round to being more effective staff members. Instead make sure that you are encouraging non-regulars to take part ("come in, the water's lovely"), while giving regular contributors enticements to avoid repeating the same old chestnuts and coming up with something new.

TIMEOUT

Failure – Shockley

William Shockley, a 1956 physics Nobel prize winner, described the development of the transistor at Bell Labs in 1948 as a "creative failure methodology." The team at Bell Labs actually failed to develop the product they had aimed to develop but ended up with the junction transistor. From this work comes the ability to develop large scale integrated circuits and, indirectly, the computers on which this book was typed.

■ Innovative Internet

Everyone knows, do they not, that the Internet is the place to be on the electronic front. This is where the cyber-happenings happen, isn't it? Well, yes and no. The Internet is a widely misunderstood concept. In part this is because it does not exist.

Confused? How can something which is mentioned every week in the media, which has had more books written about it than the British royal family, which has become such an important buzz word, not exist? Because the Internet is a concept, not a service. When people talk of regulating the Internet, they are talking nonsense. Everything that's said about the Internet could equally be said about "the printed page." The printed page is a concept, a building block for books and magazines; it is not a specific publication. Similarly the Internet simply describes the fact that thousands and thousands of computers have now been connected together. Various companies (service providers) have set up the means for ordinary folk to dial into this worldwide mess; various sites have established themselves as the place to discuss a certain topic, but overall there is no structure.

Cyberquote
"Casey's virus had bored a window through the library's command ice. He punched himself through and found an infinite blue space ranged with colour-coded spheres strung on a tight grid of pale blue neon. In the non-space of the matrix, the interior of a given data construct possessed unlimited subjective dimensions … ."
William Gibson, *Neuromancer* (Grafton, 1986).

This is neither a bad nor a good thing. It makes navigation something of a nightmare, encouraging the publication of many guides both on paper and in software. Equally it gives vent to every extreme of viewpoint from the most conservative to those supplying the pornography which has so concerned those who wish to control this uncontrollable non-existent entity. (You can, of course, control the service providers, but that's a different story.)

From our viewpoint, the key features of the Internet are electronic mail, newsgroups, and the World Wide Web. The Internet acts as a vehicle for electronic mail that can be used in the manner we've already described. Newsgroups are actually bulletin boards, rather like the ones in Lotus Notes. They cover pretty well every topic under the sun, and there's no reason for not tapping into this resource. However, it is wise to be aware that regular Internet users are often fiercely defensive of their particular areas and suspicious of business users, concerned that the free and easy ethos of the Internet will be swamped by commercialism. This concern is so strong that it smacks of paranoia. It is essential if you take this approach that you are well aware of your "netiquette," reading up one of the appropriate documents, usually available on-line from your service provider.

There is a newsgroup dedicated to creativity which is well worth having a look at: **misc.creativity**. For broader information on creativity, see the creativity World Wide Web suggestions listed below.

Creativity web sites bring together a whole welter of information on techniques, books and software and are an essential source. In fact, the Internet's sheer diversity and lack of true structure can prove an inspiration when new ideas flag. If you have access to the World Wide Web, this maze of hypertext can prove a help next time ideas fail to flow. Rather than using a creativity technique, try going to one of the "hot page" sites that regularly point to new or bizarre places. Take a look at what you find, and search for ways that you can employ the ideas, concepts, graphics – anything you see – in your problem solving or idea generation.

You could also use the Web yourself. Most Internet Service Providers offer facilities to put your own pages on the web. You

World Wide Web

Originally developed by CERN to provide a discussion environment for their particle research, the World Wide Web has become remarkably popular, providing the ease of hypertext, linking from computer to computer across the Internet.

Hypertext

Term devised by Ted Nelson to describe documents where items have automatic links to enable easy browsing.

Mining the Internet

For a practical guide to finding your way around the Internet see Brian Clegg's *Mining the Internet* (Kogan Page, 1999).

could use this to get input on a problem from the Internet community.

Web sites come and go, but here are a few suggestions for finding out more about creativity from the World Wide Web:

Creativity Unleashed
  http://www.cul.co.uk
The Australian Creativity site
  http://www.ozemail.com.au/~caveman/creative
Right Brain Works
  http://www.gocreate.com
Lucia's Creative Links
  http://www.minorkey.com/awlinks.html
Directed Creativity
  http://www.directedcreativity.com

Aerial survey

Forgotten what they're like? Check out p. 36.

Imagination Engineering

Not sure where to start? Use the map on p. 112 as a guide.

Modem

Short for modulator/de-modulator. Box or card for a PC which converts data into a format which can be transmitted down a conventional telephone line.

■ Feeling blank?

The previous page makes use of a common feature of older computer manuals, which had to be updated so frequently without sophisticated reformatting that blank sides were a common occurrence. It has been argued that these pages made more sense than practically anything else in the manual.

Here it serves a different purpose. We would like you to go back to that page now and draw yourself a brief aerial survey on what Imagination Engineering is about. There are several reasons for this. Firstly, it will serve as a useful reminder. Secondly, you were in danger of falling into the wrong mindset – if you don't have a computer about your person there's not enough exercise in this chapter.

Thirdly, we want you to challenge one of your own creativity blockers. Most of us find it quite difficult to scribble in a printed book. We have been trained since very early childhood that only specially identified books are for drawing in – anything else is vandalism. So not only do you get some exercise, you can break out of one of the many restraints that surround your every action.

■ So how do I get it?

If you are yet to experience the joys of networked creativity, it is surprisingly easy to get started. What was once the realm of the technically initiated is now within the capabilities of everyone. There are plenty of books and advice available, so we will limit ourselves to a simple approach.

To start with, you will need a personal computer and a modem or other means of connection to the Internet. While modems were once the only way of connecting, look into the faster ISDN digital telephone lines or ultra-fast methods like cable modems and ADSL before deciding. It would help if your PC was running Windows (or was an Apple). If you haven't already got a modem, try your local computer superstore or have a flick through the magazines on the news rack and find one with a comparative review of modems and other connection technology.

TIMEOUT

Creativity blockers – job specialization

Since the dawn of time man has perfected job specialization. Adam Smith, the 18th century father of political economics, saw job specialization as the defining characteristic of modern economies. Most of the wealth of modern society is created by job specialization.

This wealth creator does have its dark side. We hear it in the cry, "It's not my job!" Even where its effects are subtler it exists. We think of business problems in terms of the jobs affected by them. Our own specialization in business has helped to structure our thinking processes. The way we think about the business world is shaped by our role in it and the path we have taken through it.

In World War Two the allied forces relied quite heavily on "the back room boys," the scientists who helped to push forward the war effort. One of the sources of their creative success was the mullet-disciplinary approach which they adopted. Problems were not defined as Physics, Chemistry, Maths, Biology etc. but covered the whole span. The solutions which were generated were, as a consequence, off-the-wall – and remarkably effective.

Creative spell checker

When spell checking this box we accidentally let a correction slip through. The checker doesn't like "multi-" and converted "multidisciplinary" to "mullet-disciplinary." This term oozes with creative potential.

Once you have the equipment you will need an Internet Service Provider. These companies provide connection to the Internet via permanently linked computers. Shop around, as the business models vary widely from a subscription with free telephone calls to free connection with charged calls. If available, most people find unmetered services where there is no time-based element to the charge for connection or the call best.

Flaming

The impersonal nature of electronic communications makes it tempting to go beyond the limits we impose on face-to-face communication. In the on-line world, flaming is attacking another user's views or actions in a vitriolic fashion.

Key words

Tool; local program; network; Internet; World Wide Web.

Whichever route you choose, take your time; browse around and familiarize yourself with the way things are done before jumping in. Once you are happy with the way things work, go for it – some of the denizens of the electronic world are weird, but despite the unpleasant stories of flaming, most are friendly.

One final tip – watch your connect time. On-line services are notorious for consuming phone time. If your local calls are free, bear in mind that you are blocking incoming calls. Can you use a dedicated line or divert to another number? If you pay, remember the clock, but also remember what you are trying to do; one good idea, one major problem solved, will be worth a good few hours on the phone.

Coming soon ➤ ➤ ➤

Although there's nothing in Imagination Engineering that can't be used by someone working on their own, and some techniques positively benefit from a spot of isolation, there is also much to be gained from the ability to bounce ideas off others. We've already considered institutionalizing creativity – next we'll be looking at facilitating a group which is specifically convened to be creative.

LEAK

By Brian Martin

TALE PIECE

"That was fascinating," said Stephen Capel. He looked around the office, uncertain where his host intended him to sit. There was an austere visitor's chair by the desk, but he preferred the look of a clutch of black leather armchairs that squatted comfortably around a low coffee table.

"You're very diplomatic, reverend." Irwin Weinstadt, the managing director of Lector Limited, still had a trace of an American accent, but twenty years of living in Britain, a country which he loved with a passion that he was incapable of explaining, had smoothed it to a burr. "It can't have been very exciting."

Capel winced visibly at the "reverend." He got called many things as a Church of England vicar, few of which he actively enjoyed. "Just Capel, please. I'm not being polite, I am genuinely interested. Before I started this job I was in the civil service, mostly with the DTI."

"A new boy?"

"Almost. This is my first parish, though I did a stint as a prison chaplain. I'm rather surprised to find you on my patch. Even light industry seems out of place around Thornton Down."

"We're very careful about not upsetting our neighbors."

"I wasn't complaining, I …" Capel broke off as the door swung open accompanied by a delicate knock.

"Would you like tea?" It was Weinstadt's secretary, a woman in her twenties with short cropped, dark hair. Capel had spoken to her briefly when he arrived, but she had been typing when they returned from the tour of the plant.

"Coffee, please," said Capel. "If it's not too much trouble. I don't drink tea."

"More fool you," said Weinstadt. "Call yourself British? Fiona will be worried now; she only makes tea in the afternoon."

"I don't mind going without if it's an inconvenience," said Capel.

"It was a joke," said Weinstadt. "Fiona likes things neatly ordered, is all. In fact she's the best secretary I ever had. She's careful, she's thoughtful and she loves the job. Okay, her typing's slow and she moves her lips when she reads and she gets flustered once in a while, but that's more than made up for by the quality of her work and her enthusiasm. She's great to have around."

"Don't shoot," said Capel, holding up his hands. "I'm very impressed."

"You ought to be," said Weinstadt. There was a gentle knock and Fiona came in, carrying a tray. She smiled shyly at Capel. "I thought you might like a biscuit," she said.

 Brian Martin

Has written three detective novels featuring the very human vicar Stephen Capel. This short story was written specially for this book.

 DTI

Department of Trade and Industry: part of the UK civil service. Formed by a merger of the DOI and DOT, they wisely dropped the O in the abbreviation.

"That would be wonderful," said Capel. His particular skill was making a trivial remark seem sincere. Fiona beamed back at him.

"There was a message while you were out," she said to Weinstadt. "The bug man can't come until five."

"That's okay," said Weinstadt. "No calls for half an hour, please, Fiona."

"Trouble with cockroaches?" Capel said. "Sorry, not very tactful."

"An altogether different variety," said Weinstadt. "We've got a real problem …" He paused and took a sip of the tea. "She warms the pot, you know. How many secretaries warm the pot? You don't want to know my problems."

Capel shrugged. "It goes with the uniform."

"In our line of business we have to keep new developments under wraps. It's all too easy to be overtaken before we've even got a product on the market. And we've got a leak. A very serious leak."

"You think your office could be bugged?"

"It happens, don't think it doesn't. Bugging's a very sophisticated, remarkably cheap business these days. We've had the place swept half a dozen times and found nothing, but we have to keep checking. There must be something; the information that's getting out has to have come from this office."

"Hmm." Capel paused to drink some coffee. "How's your security?"

"Excellent. You saw on the way in. No-one gets on site without being checked. If we'd been broken into, we'd know about it."

"So that leaves people who can get in legitimately. Any workmen – your own staff for that matter."

Weinstadt shook his head. "We thought of that. All the external people who've been in here check out. As for my own staff, I trust them. This is a small firm Rev … Capel. I hire everyone personally. We all share in the profits. They wouldn't do it."

"Perhaps I could have a quick look around your office?"

"Come on," said Weinstadt, "you came to visit, not to solve my problems. Give it a rest."

"No, really," said Capel, "I'd be happy to have a look. Working in a prison gives you a certain insight into, er, shall we say less than legitimate activities."

"It's up to you."

Capel walked over to the window; it looked out over a small garden and beyond to the magnificent sweep of tree-covered hills that surround the Kennet valley. "You've a wonderful view," he said.

"I certainly do," said Weinstadt. "I've been asked why I'm not based near London. My answer's 'just look out the window'."

Capel glanced around Weinstadt's unencumbered desk, then opened the door to the outer office. Fiona's workstation was squeezed between a filing

 Bug
The term "bug" for a listening device probably originates from the idea of a fly on the wall. It has long been alleged that the same term, applied to computer programs, dated to the discovery of a moth shorting out a computer. While this event occurred (and the bug in question is taped into the computer's log book), "bug" had already been used as slang for a technical problem in engineering circles for many years.

cabinet and the outer door. "You look cramped," he said to her.

"It's not bad," said Fiona. "I couldn't work with my back to Mr Weinstadt's office, and we have to avoid the window."

"Fiona hasn't such a great outlook," said Weinstadt. He pointed to the three storey car park that filled the view from the outer office window. "They ought never to have been allowed to build it, it's an eyesore."

Capel brushed the carpet with his toe. "You turned her desk around so the PC screen wasn't visible?"

Weinstadt smiled. "Nice thought, but wrong. We moved the desks a couple of years ago when we went onto personal computers, but it was to avoid glare on the screen. The leaks came later."

Capel nodded. He squeezed past a cabinet to look over Fiona's shoulder at the computer. "Windows?" he said.

"Yes, but not the latest version," said Fiona.

Capel grinned. He had only recently been introduced to the capabilities of computers. "That's the limit of my expertise. I thought I was being clever recognizing Windows." He half turned to Weinstadt. "What about hackers?"

Weinstadt groaned. He perched on the corner of Fiona's desk and peered into the depths of his black tea. "I blame the media," he said. "You'd think that every computer in the land was in danger of being violated. To be able to hack in, they'd need to dial us up. We don't have a modem: our computer's not connected to a phone, so you can't ring in, you can't hack it. Simple as that."

"I see," said Capel. He watched the words form on Fiona's screen in silence for a while.

"And there are no monitors either," said Weinstadt, feeling a need to fill the silence.

Capel extricated himself from behind Fiona's desk and walked over to the window. The sun fell full on his face; he shaded his eyes and continued to stare into the distance, looking but not seeing. "Monitors?"

"The bug man checked last visit. You can put a gadget on a computer cable that monitors the keys that are pressed, then reproduces them elsewhere. There's nothing of that sort."

"Has all the leaked material been written on Fiona's machine?"

"I believe so."

Capel felt the hairs on the back of his neck bristling as if an insect was dancing across them. He was unable to stop his hand going up to brush away the non-existent pest. He turned slowly to face Weinstadt. "Of course," he said. "It's not the hands at all."

"Would you like to come back into my office?" Weinstadt frowned. "I've taken up too much of your time already."

"Or rather I have of yours," said Capel. He did not move his position, staring fixedly in front of him.

 Hacker
Hackers were originally quick and dirty computer programmers who "hacked" at their code rather than delicately crafting it. It only later took on the meaning of those seeking to gain unauthorized access to systems.

"No, really. I've got some brochures for you to take with you."

"Thanks; thanks very much." Capel seemed to shake off an invisible net. "After you." He followed Weinstadt into his office and sat squarely in one of the leather chairs. "It's a neat little problem."

"Please," said Weinstadt, "let's change the subject. I wasn't expecting you to solve my mystery."

"Listen for a moment," said Capel. "Humor me. Vicars are allowed to be eccentric, it's traditional. When you talked about monitors *I thought*, they can't see the screen from the car park, but what about the keyboard. Fiona doesn't type particularly quickly ..."

"I prefer quality to breakneck speed and carelessness," said Weinstadt. He sounded defensive.

"I'm not criticizing her, just stating a fact. It would be possible to watch her fingers and deduce what she's typing."

"It's possible," said Weinstadt slowly.

"No it's not." Capel sounded irritatingly cheerful. "You can't see the keyboard from the window. I checked. It's hidden by the screen."

"Forgive me, but why are you telling me this?"

"You can't see the keyboard, you can't see Fiona's hands at work, that's true, but you can see her face. Her mouth. You told me yourself, Mr Weinstadt. She moves her lips when she reads. Lipreading's by no means perfect, but it would be enough to get the gist. Enough to upset your plans. Don't you think?"

"Fiona ..." Weinstadt sounded devastated.

"She won't lose her job?" said Capel.

"Of course not," said Weinstadt. "Like I said, she's the perfect secretary. But some blinds might come in useful. And maybe before we get them I could have her type some misleading garbage. Give the opposition something to think about."

"I hope you aren't planning deception," said Capel with a broad smile.

"Would I, Capel? Would I do that?"

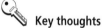 **Key thoughts**

- Try looking in a totally different direction
- Be prepared to drop failed ideas quickly – but build on them.

GROUP CREATIVITY

Facilitation

If you decide to facilitate groups yourself, see Tony Spinks and Phil Clements, *Practical Guide to Facilitation Skills* (Kogan Page, 1993).

Consulting

A linked theme, particularly around the role of the facilitator, is covered in Peter Block, *Flawless Consulting* (Pfeiffer, 1981).

INTRODUCTION

The techniques we are describing in this book work well if you are alone or part of a group. Although there are times when solitude is necessary for really creative thought, creativity often sparks more readily in a group. Try both solo and group creativity. Try each for different problems and in different settings. See what works for you.

If you do work in a group, make sure that you have the group facilitated. A facilitator helps the meeting process while staying out of the content. Group creativity sessions which are facilitated work better than ones which are not. If you are unable or unwilling to bring in an experienced facilitator, this chapter gives a brief introduction to those who take on the role for themselves.

ROLE OF THE FACILITATOR

A facilitator has no formal power. They are there to control the process of the meeting (*how* the meeting takes place) and need to stay out of the content of the meeting (*what* is taking place). The lack of formal power means that the facilitator directs the meeting with the consent of the participants. If they decide not to legitimize the facilitator, they can take the meeting away and redirect it.

A facilitator suggests methods and procedures for progressing. It is essential, for instance, that the person facilitating a creativity group understands the creative process and the techniques available for enhancing creativity. More than this, they need to have an understanding of the way groups of people work, and need to understand the tools and techniques specific to facilitation.

A facilitator protects individuals and ideas. It is so easy to destroy a creative idea generating session with a remark or an observation made in the wrong way or at the wrong time. If this is seen as an attack on an individual or an idea, then the contributor will clam up. Worse than this, they will look for an opportunity for revenge. The revenge is often far more savage than the original attack. If you don't believe that the people you work with would behave in this way, just watch. Once you notice a critical remark directed at a person or one of their ideas, watch that person and wait for the revenge. You will usually not have to wait long.

A facilitator encourages participation. A fundamental rule of creativity sessions is that they start with a number of ideas, and avoid trying to impose a spurious concept of quality at a stage where it simply doesn't apply. If some of the group are not contributing fully then some ideas are being lost. Those with the widest mouths do not necessarily make the best contributions.

PROCESS VERSUS CONTENT

We have said that the facilitator stays out of the content and monitors and directs the process. It is equally important that the creative thinkers forget the process and immerse themselves in the content. If participants are worrying about where a particular avenue of thought is taking them or when the next coffee break might be, they are not giving their all to the content. For this reason, it's useful to make sure that the participants understand and are comfortable with the process (including when the coffee breaks are – never underestimate the physical) before beginning. The facilitator needs to ensure that closure is achieved in these matters.

The inputs that a facilitator makes during the meeting are called interventions. They are about redirecting the process. The more skilled a facilitator becomes, the less they feel a need to intervene. Initially it is tempting as a facilitator to direct every moment of a meeting. The feeling is that unless you are actively involved you are not doing anything, but this is a particularly Zen role. Less is very definitely more.

Closure
The process of mentally checking off a task or thought as completed, so it does not continue to nag from the back of the mind.

Creativity blockers – "I am not creative"

This is the biggest creativity blocker you are likely to hit, in yourself or in others. The Pygmalion Effect ensures that if you believe something is true, you will act as though it were true. If you believe something is true about you, you will not only act as though it were true, you will make it true. If

 TIMEOUT

you believe you are not creative then you are right. Similarly, if you believe that you are creative then you are right.

The exercises in this book should demonstrate that with the application of simple techniques you can increase your ability to generate creative solutions. Apply those techniques consistently for a short time and you will not only be generating creative solutions, you will become creative. Then comes the hardest step of all, believing in yourself. We have very little practical help here. Our hope is that once you start to see the results you are able to produce, the last step will come about by itself.

PREVENTION IS BETTER THAN CURE

 Preparation

Find the next large meeting in your diary. Even if you don't have a facilitating role, practice being prepared by spending five minutes sketching out the preparation described here.

Facilitating a group session involves far more than turning up and doing a good job on the day. A creativity session (like any meeting) starts long before people get together and ends long after. Work on process before the meeting prevents the need for redirection during the meeting.

Identify the owner of the problem or the person who will be responsible for implementing the idea. Ensure that they are at the meeting. Spend time with them before the session understanding what they want, why they want it and how they want to get there. Agree with them what you will and will not do, what you can and cannot achieve. Every minute spent planning the session at this stage prevents one or two potential problems in the session itself.

Next, identify the attendees of the session. They are the resources that you can use as facilitator to achieve the objectives of the sponsor or owner of the meeting. You may need to talk to some of these people before the meeting but usually only if there are political tensions or likely implementation issues which need to be addressed.

Before the meeting starts make a few general statements about what you will be doing, how you will go about it and what you expect of the participants. Clarity here will pay dividends later.

INTERVENTIONS

Intervening in the direction of a meeting should be done with a light touch. Before doing anything, ask yourself if it is really necessary. If you decide to intervene, consider using body language rather than words. A nod of the head, holding a hand up, turning yourself towards or away from someone, and most of all, eye contact, can all be very powerful. If you have a chance to watch an experienced facilitator then take it and observe what they do. If you have a chance to watch yourself on video then take that too. It can be embarrassing when you see yourself doing dumb things but it is extremely enlightening.

We have found that the most obvious interventions you need to make are the ones which involve changing the pace or the state of a meeting. When people are slowing down and drilling their rear ends deeper and deeper into their chairs then you need to get them up and about. Get them moving around. Generate some energy. When you are losing attention because it is all getting too raucous then slow things down a little by having a quieter, more reflective activity. Develop a tool bag of games and activities which you can use to change pace. Some of our favorites include:

- **The armory** – a bag of weapons, such as water pistols, soft rubber balls and other projectiles. This is useful for loosening up an otherwise tight or starchy group. Weapons can be used in a whole range of situations, most frequently for limiting evaluation of ideas. Evaluate and be drenched.

- **Up and moving activities** – a series of team games, such as building the tallest tower with a newspaper and a roll of tape, or passing a ball between team members without using your hands. These have nothing to do with the session itself but work well when you need a change of pace. Whatever you do, keep these asides short – they are about enhancing the idea generation, not replacing it.

- **Slowing down activities** – sitting thinking, working on your own, writing down your own ideas on a sheet of paper, working on individual puzzles – all of these work well to slow down the pace. They also give the facilitator time to collect their thoughts and prepare for the next stage of the session.

 Warm-up

At the next long meeting you are responsible for, warm up the participants with a fun exercise. Ask everyone to write down which animal best represents them, and why. Then have them read back their answers. You might also ask for an animal to represent the group and your company.

Warm-up medley

For a collection of over seventy warm-ups and other exercises to get energy into groups see Brian Clegg and Paul Birch's *Instant Teamwork* (Kogan Page, 1998).

OBSTACLES AND DIFFICULTIES

You will not always have perfect creativity sessions. Some groups will work well and others will not. This may or may not be your responsibility, but as facilitator you should look after yourself as well as the meeting. Don't take difficulties personally. Learn from them. Do what you can to prevent them next time.

You will have difficult participants. There will be people who believe that they know better than you the way things should be run. Talk to them, ideally one to one but with the whole group if necessary. Explain that you are there to run the process and intend to do the best you can but that you need their consent for that to happen. If you cannot make this work then the ultimate position is for you to step away. If you cannot make a session work you are better admitting that than struggling on and failing spectacularly. Don't give up too soon, though. With this sort of session the darkest hour often really is just before dawn.

A common reason for a creativity session to fail is the venue. Make sure that you are working in the best surroundings possible. Do not go for a room with a large, immovable table in the center. Make sure that you have plenty of space to move around, plenty of light to see what's written up, plenty of flip charts, or similar, to record ideas, and above all, plenty of refreshments in constant supply.

AFTER THE MEETING

Decide beforehand how you will close the session. Do you want feedback from the participants or not? What are you committing to do? What are others committing to do? What happens to any record of the meeting? Who writes up what, how and in what form? What results come out of the meeting? Who takes them further and how? Make sure that this was not just a fun interlude. Make sure that it leads to productive output. But remember that this is a creativity session. Don't make the minutes a tedious list of what was set and a checklist of action points. Make it readable and fun. A challenge? Certainly. Impossible? No.

Cliché corner

Clichés are wonderful things: sometimes they are repetitive (each and every), sometimes uneconomical (why say "in the vicinity of" when you can say "near?"). "The darkest hour is just before dawn" is a striking cliché, because not only is it a metaphor, but it's a metaphor based on an untrue premise.

Fun minutes

Think back to the last meeting you attended. Construct a set of minutes which reflect what happened, but are fun to read. Use layout, pictures, whatever is needed. Think about how the meeting would be described in a tabloid newspaper – they can't afford to be boring.

TIMEOUT

Thomas Alva Edison

Thomas Edison is remembered as one of the most prolific inventors of the 20th century. He patented over 1,000 new inventions. His firm belief was that, "there is no substitute for hard work." This belief led directly to his most famous quote, "Genius is 1 percent inspiration and 99 percent perspiration."

Edison credited his inventing success to the fact that he did not wait to be struck by an idea but set out to find it. He would often decide what he wanted to invent before knowing if it was possible. He would then work on ways of developing the product that he had envisaged.

Coming soon ➤➤➤

Techniques can only take you so far. In the penultimate chapter, we look at moving beyond techniques, towards holistic creativity. This tale piece considers holistic copying, an altogether different prospect.

Key words
Facilitation: process, not content. Preparation: intervention. Afterwards: fun minutes.

TALE PIECE

BOOKENDS

By Brian Clegg

"Like a good challenge, don't you?"

"Is that a threat?" He laughs briefly.

"Have you read this?"

"Let's have a look … No, I don't bother with all this technical crap." He leaves the magazine lying limply in his lap.

"Read it. The new products section."

"I will, don't worry. Have you been working late again?"

"When you're my age you'll cope better with being patronizing. Read it now. I can wait."

The visitor – our man – sits back further in his chair and sighs. The old boy must have had a bad weekend; now he needs to take it out on a junior. Our man didn't go into publishing to grub around in the fiddly details of how it works. He flicks through the magazine – poorly printed, it's amazing they stay in business – glances casually at the article. His shoulders ease back involuntarily and the short hairs on the back of his beautifully groomed neck bristle. He starts the article again, studying it word for word.

Copying Breakthrough Announced

The first copier capable of reproducing an entire book in one pass was demonstrated at a press conference in New York yesterday. The Hyoceron Corporation of Japan has spent five years perfecting the technology, which can reproduce a five hundred page volume in less than a minute.

"We expect to go into full production by the end of the second quarter," said Mark Stradler, US CX of Hyoceron. "Our product will revolutionize the copying business. In a matter of seconds, and at a trivial cost, an entire report can be reproduced, without the tedious mechanical effort of sorting and collating."

The Holistic copier works by using a form of laser X-ray. The three-dimensional scan is effected by using a reference X-ray source and a scanning source, which combine to form a refraction pattern, in the same way that a conventional hologram is formed.

Printing is worked by a similar process in reverse, enabling a stack of paper (which can be pre-bound in book form) to be printed at one shot. Variable costs are limited to the price of stationery.

Although Hyoceron have a clear lead at the moment, it is unlikely that the other copier manufacturers will be far behind. Somehow, reproduction may never be the same again.

As he reads, panic speeds up his eyes, driving them faster than his brain can absorb information, so that the last paragraphs are skipped. He forces himself to go back once more and take in every detail.

"Give me an hour." He walks to his office. Walks, floats – gets there somehow. His secretary says something but he does not hear. Inside the office he sits at his desk and pulls forward a huge blank pad. Our man thinks best with a pen in his hand.

 Thinking with a pen

You will often be more creative if you do your thinking with a pen in your hand, not to make formal structured notes, but to doodle, mind map and scrawl.

Seventy minutes later he is back. The old man has somehow managed to pull in the board – even the decrepit Greenbaum.

"Michael will give us a briefing," says the old man. No surprises here. Drop him in it and see what he comes out smelling of is the old man's standard technique for testing the ground. He has a simple philosophy. The good guys will get it right. The rest can find a job somewhere else. It's an echo of the way they treated witches in the middle ages.

"Right," our man Michael says: we know him a bit better now, we can be on first name terms. "We have six months to change this company totally or to get out of the business." That gets them talking. They don't like change in publishing. It's all about setting things down in black and white. Change is an irritation, an inconvenience.

Michael drifts away from the meeting. His mind, that is: the body stays solidly planted in the Italian shoes. We've a chance here to see a bit more of him. Not that Michael's a dreamer. The pause is quite deliberate. Let them run their course a bit. Argue amongst themselves … Our Michael has a mental alarm clock. He can go onto hold for thirty five seconds and click back in as if he was never away.

Away, for Michael, has two clear dimensions. His mind doesn't so much wander, as plot a graph. On one axis, his status. On the other, time. Time from now to the future; Michael has no interest in the past.

No prizes for guessing which way the plot goes. Today it is a bright golden line, predicting the growth in his fame as he saves the publishing house. Little crosses mark the highlights. Here, his promotion. There, the interviews with the press. Soon, the man of the year award. Nowhere, strangely, is the actual effort which wins the accolades. Only the kudos, never the sweat. Ping. His mental timer has gone off. Our period of contemplation is over.

"You don't believe me," he says, not shouting, but carrying over the fading hubbub. "Listen first. Then, if you like, ignore me and be like ostriches." He tells them about the article.

"So?" says Raitlen, the art editor. "They've made a new photocopier. Do you know how often they do that? It's a toy. Big deal."

"Wrong, Mr Raitlen, enormous deal," says Michael. Greenbaum raises an eyebrow but says nothing. He has not spoken at all yet. "This thing," says

Michael, speaking slowly, splitting word from word, talking as to children, "this thing gives us the same headaches as the music and video business have had since tapes were invented. We are talking book piracy."

"Come on," says McFadden, cocky Mr Finance, "they've been able to copy books for ages."

"Oh, sure. And how many people were going to spend two or three hours copying a book page by page? It's not worth it. But copy the whole thing – it's a different ball game. Why spend ten dollars when you can borrow a book and copy it in seconds? And, apart from the cover, the duplicate would be just as good as the original. Better – you could copy an ordinary book into a prestige shell."

"It's illegal," McFadden again. "It says quite clearly in the prelims …"

Michael does not need to reply. He looks sadly at McFadden and continues. "But it's not all bad. We'll keep some business, anything with color illustrations. It didn't say in the article, but I can't believe they can do this economically in color. Look at color photocopiers: too expensive.

"And suppose we turn this idea on its head. For fiction, we've got a chance to use it. Imagine a new type of bookshop – they have one copy only of each book they carry, no need to have separate stocks with different covers. Or multiple copies of best-sellers, so they have a better range of stock. They also have a copier and different blanks for paperbacks and the quality merchandise. They make the book, they don't just sell it. If people want, they can have personalized covers … anything."

"You think the opportunities outweigh the dangers?" The old man is not convinced.

"Do we have a choice? Maybe I overplayed the problem; people aren't going to have these things in the home. Piracy will be down to professionals, and people doing a bit on the side in the office. But I still say it's going to turn the business upside down. And the opportunities are there."

"On the whole, I agree with Michael." Oh-oh. Not so good. It's Lake, the fiction editor. The token woman (right now they're an old-fashioned firm). Hates his guts. Always ready with the knife.

"The machine is a threat," she says. "And I always hold Michael's judgement in high esteem. I'm sure he has thought through his idea in great detail. But, with the greatest respect …" here it comes. Slash … "he's wrong about the way we should react. We would be plunging a huge amount of capital into an impossible scheme. How do you control it – and make sure that we get the revenue? What's in it for the shops, other than ripping us off? What happens when the copier breaks? We're stumbling into virgin territory and it's loaded with risk."

You should know about virgin territory, thinks Michael. She is a target where his mind graph doesn't show a steady climb. There's a little cross marked Lake and there the line droops.

He rallies; this isn't the time for a pause, he needs a triumphant close. "Of course there's risk. You don't win by waiting for everyone else. If we get in first and supply the bookshops, we control the outlets. We're going to change from a second-rate press to the leaders of the game. We can do it."

He sits down, feeling victorious. They will talk and worry the idea for a while, but they will come round to his way of thinking. He feels the old man's chair, crying out for him to occupy it. As the meeting breaks up, Greenbaum calls him over. If Michael wasn't so pleased with himself, he'd probably tell the old bastard where to go. It's time somebody did. The company, the new company, has no time for the past.

Greenbaum pokes at the magazine which he has been fussing with during most of the discussion.

"It says they'll be ready by the end of the second quarter. Does that give us enough time for your grandiose plans? It's only three months. You don't turn a business upside down in three months."

"We can do it. With the right people pushing this company we can make it what it ought to be."

"Perhaps. But you need to think more about timing before putting your neck too firmly on the line."

"Don't worry about me. I'm happy to let my career ride on this one. After all, I've got a long way to go."

Unlike some, he thinks, as he bounces into his office. He leans back in his chair, appearing to contemplate the wall. Contemplating a future of power for Michael. The graph climbs so steeply it goes right off the paper. The line is red now. A pulsing, glowing red. Hot enough to melt through the surface of the icy Lake. The company isn't all he's going to take.

A phone chirps.

"Mr Ford for you, sir."

He almost says no. Ford's close: you could nearly call him a friend, if you can imagine Michael with a friend. But he daren't say anything yet. Publishing makes the average sieve look watertight. Mention it in the morning and it's round the wine bars by four p.m. But he can handle it. He can handle anything.

"Put him on."

"Michael, how are you?"

"Never better, Simon. Yourself?"

"Great. We must fix dinner sometime."

"You're so right. And?"

"And?"

"You rang me. There must be more."

"Just social. Did you see that article in the Print Pro?"

Of course. Simon was an avid reader of the trade journals. Saved him from getting down to anything more strenuous. Michael was cool, neutral,

Key thoughts

- Perception is often more important than reality
- But reality wins when you think you can fly and jump off a building
- Being creative you should challenge, but try to avoid giving offence.

firmly covering a strong urge to laugh aloud. "Which was that? I scanned through the rag, but I haven't read anything in depth."

"You can't have seen it. You'd know. Christ, we've been running round like scalded cats. Put the fear of God up Slater."

"Not before time. Good, was it? Another Australian take-over bid? Or maybe a new awards ceremony?"

"I shouldn't say anything, not if you haven't read it. It would spoil the effect."

"Don't worry. It's too late, now."

"There's an article, somewhere in the first five pages. I haven't got it in front of me."

"Me neither; I'll have to look it out. I don't think I've binned it yet." Oh, so cool.

"It says they're going to bring out a machine to copy books – instantly. Slater's face was a picture."

"I can imagine. What are you going to do?" Just a hint of concern; he has to give himself time before he appears to realize the implications.

"Nothing. There's no need – that's the real killer. Somewhere on the back page, you know, the funnies section, it says in very small print that the whole article is an April 1st gag. I nearly wet myself. Two hours of sheer chaos for an April Fool's joke. Orson Welles would have been proud. You really should look it out, Michael."

Our man holds the phone away from his ear, as if he has suddenly discovered it is covered in slime. The old man set him up. The burning line on the graph has faced a mirror and retreated at a clean, precise right angle. Down, way down.

"Michael? Are you there?"

THE FUTURE
- BEYOND
TECHNIQUES

Go Rin No Sho

Miyamoto Musashi, *A Book of Five Rings* (Flamingo, 1984).

Inner creativity

Brian Clegg's book *Instant Brainpower* (Kogan Page, 1999) provides over seventy exercises for enhancing your personal creativity.

Throughout this book we have emphasized the importance of Imagination Engineering as a strong analogy that allows you to link creativity techniques, to remember them and therefore to use them. But techniques are not everything. They are the tools in your tool box, no more and no less. In response to the saying, "When all you have is a hammer everything starts to look like a nail," we have attempted to widen your range of tools. Your tools shouldn't shape the way that you use them. However, a master craftsman will be able to do a better job than a novice, almost regardless of the tools used.

In 1645 a Samurai called Miyamoto Musashi wrote a pamphlet on strategy called *Go Rin No Sho*, or *A Book of Five Rings*. Despite being written by a man who was born before the Spanish Armada set sail, it is well worth reading today. He divides his instruction into five "books." The Ground Book is a basic introduction to his school. The Water Book describes the strategy of the school in terms of the spirit. The Fire Book describes the strategy of the school in terms of physical skill. The Wind Book describes the strategies of other schools. The fifth, final, and shortest book, The Book of the Void, is the hardest to comprehend. It describes strategy in terms of the void – that which cannot be known. It is a step beyond the techniques and learning of strategy to the point where you *are* strategy. Your techniques become so internalized that they are no longer a part of your conscious thought. This is our intention with Imagination Engineering: that creativity becomes so natural an approach that it does not require conscious employment of techniques.

With regular practice you will move through phases of competence to the point where your thinking processes automatically broaden out before focussing down. The techniques will become so much a part of your thinking that you will no longer need to be aware of them. Don't rush towards this. Lean on the techniques for as long as you are more comfortable with them than without them. Always keep in the back of your mind that they are only techniques. You provide the skill and the ability, they are the tools which you use. If it is appropriate to use a particular tool then use it. If you have no need of it then do not.

Don't confuse this with an early reluctance to bother with a technique. It's time to put techniques to one side when they are no effort at all, not when they are too much trouble.

 **TIMEOUT**

> ### Save The Children Fund
>
> Asked how to make sure that the Save The Children Fund was at the top of people's minds when their collectors called, the Leo Burnett Innovations Unit set up a creativity session which included a range of springboards and excursions. The result of this activity was a giant collecting can on the back of a truck which was driven from region to region. In each region a celebrity was invited to help fill the can. The resulting, regional publicity made the job of the door-to-door collectors more effective.

 Key thoughts

- You are creative, not the techniques
- Use techniques as a tool, not a crutch
- When techniques become second nature, try to surpass them.

Coming soon ➤ ➤ ➤

Time to start looking outwards. There's nothing more dangerous than endings, so take great care. In the final chapter we pull together Imagination Engineering, but first, even if you haven't bothered to read the tale pieces up to now (shame on you), do try this one.

❡TALE PIECE

MY BOOK

By Gene Wolfe

Gene Wolfe
Is arguably the best living science fiction and fantasy writer. From his darkly mysterious *The Fifth Head of Cerberus*, through the quirky brilliance of *There Are Doors* to his equally stunning serial novels, Wolfe uses words like few other popular writers. Go out and buy some.

I have been writing my book for a long time now. In the morning, before anyone else is up, I wake to Mahler on the clock radio, shave, and go to my desk. On weekends, while the others are watching baseball, I am there too, scoring my own hits, my own runs. And in the evenings. "It keeps me off the streets," I say, though only to myself. To my manuscript. At night, when I cannot sleep, I come here too, and that is best of all. I do not hear the cry of the solitary owl; but I wish I did, which is almost as good.

Sometimes – indeed, usually – I do not write. A great deal of time is consumed by research, by planning. I heat water in my yellow electric pot, sharpen pencils, and turn over a thousand old books, most of them quite worthless. They fascinate me. Valuable books are like diamonds, iridescent and unchanging. It is in the ephemeral that I see the changing face of Nature reflected. The day darkens; the very leaves fall.

I mark certain passages in all these books, as Tom Sawyer marked similar passages in Injun Joe's Cave. It is often years before I find them again, with an archaeologist's thrill of rediscovery. No doubt there are many more I never find.

Quite recently, in an essay by Philip Rahv, I came across the passage that began it all. My writing has been influenced by many other passages: "I've progressed, in one sense, rather alarmingly. I'm now thinking of reconstructing the whole thing," by Oliver Onions, and Stout's, "It was nice to know the next step was obvious, but it would have been even nicer to know what it was." But it was this (forgotten now for so many years) that set me off: "Man is now unaware of the real powers that govern his life; insofar as he has any knowledge of divinity it is as of something purely historical." The unreeling of human history is implied, and from that thought I have taken my method. Of every book, there must be a last word as well as a first, and as the last – infinitely, in the scale of mere words, removed from the first – is also infinitely more important, I determined to write it first. I at once discovered that it scarcely mattered what it was. But after long contemplation of the book I had conceived, and somewhat, I admit, in a spirit of jocular defiance, I settled on the word *preface*.

At once I found that the whole book had changed, shifting like a kaleidoscope to become something novel and strange. The last word decided, it crystallized without solidification. The penultimate word seemed foreordained yet enigmatic: *begin*. The ending would be pregnant with the origins of things, raveling history to the finish. Everything altered again, as ice shifts upon a river, groaning, cracking in the night. I returned to find the white sheets destroyed, though each was where I had left it. I began the search for the antepenultimate word.

It was *will*, the word of purpose, the impulse that began the universe.

And then the preantepenultimate word …

And so I have proceeded, step by laborious (delightful) step, chapter by chapter, until soon, perhaps this very year, surely before the coronation, I will begin the preface.

Key thoughts

- Reversal of a sequence is a neat variant on distortion as a building technique
- Don't always fill in every detail – this story is a gem because it is so short
- And because suggestion inspires more thought than clarity – "what coronation?" – precisely
- Don't let trivia cloud a great idea. It doesn't matter that the penultimate word is the definite article.

chapter twelve

GO FORTH AND CREATE!

Apple 1984
The Apple Macintosh was hurled into the public perception by a minute-long commercial, first screened during the SuperBowl, which portrayed Apple as an athlete, breaking the Big Brother, 1984 mould of computing.

Using a creative approach once to crack a big problem brings real benefits. Using such an approach regularly not only provides more benefit, but makes creative thinking easier, more natural, and more effective.

In the end, creativity is like any other skill. Use it and it will flourish; neglect it and it will fade away. We have two real aims with this book. One is to make creativity fun. In many ways, business creativity faces the same image problems that business computing did in the early eighties. Because it was *business* computing it had to be stodgy, grey and boring. So went conventional thinking. But Apple Computer came along and blew this image out of the water just as surely as its 1984 TV advertisement was a landmark for TV advertising.

Although Apple themselves have never really taken hold of the corporate heart and mind, their legacy is the way that computers at the heart of business have seen a transformation on their screens as Microsoft Windows has grown from shaky early beginnings to become a fun way of working. It never should have been any different. Computers can deliver exciting things – they have no reason to be dull.

Similarly, by its very nature, creativity ought to be the most thrilling aspect of business. Yet the desire to be respected as professional and establishment has led many practitioners to make the subject as dull as ditchwater. We don't want it to be that way, and we hope that comes across.

Our other aim is to make applied creativity – Imagination Engineering – part of your everyday life. That's the point of Imagination Engineering. Not to add an extra layer of complexity, but to give you a memory handle to cope with the techniques that make the whole process work.

Remember the simple four headings: **surveying, building, way-marking, navigating**. But we've been scathing about the check box approach to implementation. Should we resort to a checklist to help reinforce Imagination Engineering ideas, or is there something better? Perhaps the decision ought to be down to you. We're going to tell you a little story, the whole point of which is to push the ideas of Imagination Engineering more firmly into your mind. Images help to fix ideas into long-term memory: hopefully this story will do this for you. This is not a tale piece, it is an exercise.

Our journey will be undertaken by a fat, purple pig. See him on top of a hill, **surveying** the directions he has to go. He thinks he wants to go to the funfair. Just to be sure, he gets out his **compass**. It's big and brass. He asks **why** am I going there? For fun. And **why** does he want to have fun? Because he's going to be made into bacon tomorrow. As he looks around he notices an **obstacle** in his way. He draws himself a little picture on a handy cheeseburger.

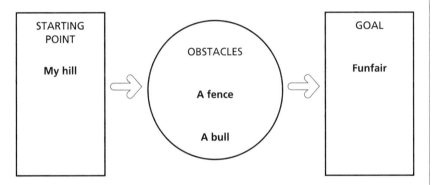

The bull roars at him.

Irritated, the pig decides to think of a new way of getting along without going through the bull's field. He uses his **level chain** to move away from the idea of fields, **up** to counties then back **down** to county towns, trunk roads and elephants. He decides to ride through the bull's field on an elephant. But the elephant, which has been playing with a big, red, helium balloon, breathes it all in and floats over the field like a blimp, giving the pig a bird's eye view of the area – an **aerial survey**. He draws a quick map in his mind so he will know where to go. Now he is clear about his **destination**, he wants to know **how to get to** the funfair. Or he might not go at all. **With no destination**, how could he still have fun?

He decides to make the journey. His balloon landed on the wrong side of the bull, so he needs to **build** a solution. Using a sharpened salami he digs a tunnel. In his **tunnel** he finds that his **assumption** that the ground was made of earth is wrong. Actually it is marshmallow. His vision **distorts**: the field is not 20 meters across but 20 kilometers. And, strangest of all, a **reversal**, he isn't digging with the salami, it is digging with him.

He wipes marshmallow out of his nostrils and backs up. Another solution, then. He **fantasizes** that a hundred naked sows pile themselves up to act as a **bridge** – only they don't. Of course, if he took another **point of view** – the bull's – or arrived before the bull was there he could cross easily. Of course, **metaphorically**, the bull is like a competitor for the trotter of Rosy, his favorite lady pig, but he can't get round it by sending chocolates (truffles, of course).

Perhaps he should go round the field, **by-passing** it altogether. He could probably do that using a thumb-screw (a **word** picked at **random**): he **pictures** the thumb-screw fixed firmly on the tail of his business rival, Porky. It's as if he can really see the **object** of torture. But then, that's **nonsense**: Porky hasn't got a tail, he's a guinea pig.

Failing that, he wonders if he should pick a **new destination**. He'd quite like to go to the moon, if only a pig could fly – but that's **fantasy**. On the other hand, there's another fair in the opposite direction.

With all these possibilities, it's time to do some **waymarking**. He puts all his ideas on the ground and rolls on them in the mud until it's very slippery and he slides in one direction – his **slip road**. This is the solution he will take. He pauses in the **washroom** (remember he's a purple pig – visualize a purple pig in an elegant ladies' washroom) to examine his **feelings** (we'll leave the image here up to you). Some lady vampire killers come in, carrying their equipment. He asks these **stakeholders** their **viewpoints**.

They point out the **good aspects** of the signpost saying no pigs. And **warn** him of the **hazard** of where they'll stick their stakes if he doesn't make a swift exit.

When he comes out of the washroom he is ready to **navigate** to the funfair. He has to choose between the wonderful steam **railway**, driven by Lawrence the Lion, or driving himself down the **highway** in his pink Cadillac, or cruising the **country lanes** in his Range Rover, or taking a paddle boat down the **river**.

Should he be **flexible** and turn up without booking or agree a detailed itinerary with a travel agent to **check** the **boxes** for him (boxes of warm tapioca). He decides to just go, but lists what he's got to do by spelling out the letters with voles. With the **tasks** in place for his **journey plan**, he checks he's got his **portable phone** to call the AA (Animal Association) for **help**. He checks the **milestones** where he's going to pause for a little snack of ripe garbage, **fixes times** to set off again and leaves for the funfair. It's a shame that ten minutes later he was run over by a steamroller, and left as a purple blot in the road. But that's life.

You are probably fed up with us telling you to go back by now, but here it comes for one last time. The trouble with memory techniques is working up the mental impetus to use them. You've probably come across the party game where a circle of people relate what is in their bag, each adding a new item to the list as the turn passes from player to player. I tried this once using the simple memory technique of building a little story and incorporating each element as new items were added to the imaginary bag. At the end of the game, when everyone else had totally lost track, I still had a perfect list. However, usually I don't bother to use the technique. Although it takes a bare minimum of effort, it doesn't get used.

Similarly, the story above will help you remember creativity techniques, but only if you read it word for word. Don't skip, plough through it, taking everything in. If it doesn't quite work for you, reconstruct the story with your own images (you can make them much more personal and raunchy than we can).

Because you are the customer, and you might still feel more comfortable this way, we're also including a checklist. It's unnecessary, it doesn't work very well, but here goes:

Memory

Using the rhyming words 1=gun, 2=shoe, 3=tree, 4=door, 5=hive, 6=sticks, 7=heaven, 8=weight, 9=sign, 0 =hole (think oh) pick a telephone number out of the book. String the objects together to form a strong sequence, adding color and drama. Once the sequence is clearly established, leave it alone. Come back next morning – most people will still remember the number.

Surveying

- Compass – Why? Why? Why?
- Something in the way? Obstacle map
- New idea? Level chain
- Aerial survey
- Destination – How to get to ... or no destination at all

Building

- Tunnel – challenge assumptions, distort facts, reverse relations
- Bridge – fantasy, different point of view or time, metaphor
- By-pass – random word or picture, objects, nonsense
- New destination – fantasy, second choice

Waymarking

- Slip road – picking off solutions
- Washroom – what's it feel like?
- Viewpoints – what do others think of it?
- Signposts – what's good about it?
- Hazard markers – how to fix what's wrong with it

Navigating

- Railway, highway, country lane or river
- Flexible or check box
- Journey plan
- Tasks
- Time boxes or project plans
- Milestones
- Packing your bag – mobile phone

The only way to get lasting benefit from Imagination Engineering is to use it and go on using it. Not tomorrow, not next week, but now. Make a conscious effort to use it in your business decisions and idea sessions. We would also recommend setting aside a short time – fifteen minutes will do – each week to be driven by creativity. Put a regular slot in your diary, and when it comes round, go through a full Imagination Engineering exercise on anything that is currently of interest to you, work or not. In chapter 2 we gave you some warm-up exercises. In music and sport, for example, even the best professional performer continues to practice throughout their career – so must you.

Finally, remember how much creativity is stimulated by external influences. If you are working on a major undertaking, whether solving a problem, generating an idea or starting a new line of business, make sure there is breathing space in the work – space where you can not only get away from the specific tasks, but be distracted by something else. A fifteen minute fiction break mid-afternoon can be an excellent stimulus. Even a business book can be effective if it's not a textbook. Try one of the popularized accounts of a business hero's rise to fame. Or if you're working in a group, have a coffee and doughnuts break and talk about sport, or cars, or television – anything but work. If you get criticized for non-productive time, laugh – this is one of your most productive times, you just haven't recorded the output yet.

 **TIMEOUT**

More alive

Asked to help develop a lively, positive theme for communication on healthy eating by one of the UK bodies concerned with promoting health, the Leo Burnett Innovations Unit ran a creativity session which resulted in the strap line, "Simply more alive" with each letter i being a leaping figure. The idea was not used, which demonstrates that even good creative ideas may end up not being implemented.

Key words

Regular creativity; fun and remembering; the purple pig; take a break.

Coming soon ➤ ➤ ➤

A must-read tale piece and the index. That's all: otherwise it's up to you. Boredom, inflexibility and doing it the way it's always been done – or excitement, flexibility and creativity. Oh, and risk too. But who said life wasn't going to be risky?

FROM THROUGH THE LOOKING GLASS AND WHAT ALICE FOUND THERE

By Lewis Carroll

There was a short silence after this, and then the Knight went on again. "I'm a great hand at inventing things. Now, I daresay you noticed, that last time you picked me up, that I was looking rather thoughtful?"

"You *were* a little grave," said Alice.

"Well, just then I was inventing a new way of getting over a gate – would you like to hear it?"

"Very much indeed," Alice said politely.

"I'll tell you how I came to think of it," said the Knight.

"You see, I said to myself, 'The only difficulty is with the feet: the *head* is high enough already.' Now, first I put my head on the top of the gate – then I stand on my head – then the feet are high enough, you see – then I'm over, you see."

"Yes, I suppose you'd be over when that was done," Alice said thoughtfully: "but don't you think it would be rather hard?"

"I haven't tried it yet," the Knight said, gravely: "so I can't tell for certain – but I'm afraid it *would* be a little hard."

He looked so vexed at the idea, that Alice changed the subject hastily. "What a curious helmet you've got!" she said cheerfully. "Is that your invention too?"

The Knight looked down proudly at his helmet, which hung from the saddle. "Yes," he said, "but I've invented a better one than that – like a sugar loaf. When I used to wear it, if I fell off the horse, it always touched the ground directly. So I had a *very* little way to fall, you see – But there *was* the danger of falling *into* it, to be sure. That happened to me once – and the worst of it was, before I could get out again, the other White Knight came and put it on. He thought it was his own helmet."

The Knight looked so solemn about it that Alice did not dare to laugh. "I'm afraid you must have hurt him," she said in a trembling voice, "being on the top of his head."

"I had to kick him, of course," the Knight said, very seriously. "And then he took the helmet off again – but it took hours and hours to get me out. I was as fast as – as lightning, you know."

"But that's a different kind of fastness," Alice objected.

The Knight shook his head. "It was all kinds of fastness with me, I can assure you!" he said. He raised his hands in some excitement as he said this, and instantly rolled out of the saddle, and fell headlong into a deep ditch.

Alice ran to the side of the ditch to look for him. She was rather startled

♪ TALE PIECE

Background

Alice has just witnessed a battle between the Red and White Knights and is left in the company of the White Knight.

Confusion technique

The White Knight's confusion of the two meanings of fast (in Victorian times the use of "fast" to mean stuck was common) provides a nice variant on a building technique. It won't always work, but is there a word in your destination statement which can be misinterpreted? Try it on some earlier examples.

by the fall, as for some time he had kept on very well, and she was afraid that he really was *hurt* this time. However, though she could see nothing but the soles of his feet, she was much relieved to hear that he was talking on in his usual tone. "All kinds of fastness," he repeated: "but it was careless of him to put another man's helmet on – with the man in it, too."

"How *can* you go on talking so quietly, head downwards?" Alice asked, as she dragged him out by the feet, and laid him in a heap on the bank.

The Knight looked surprised at the question. "What does it matter where my body happens to be?" he said. "My mind goes on working all the same. In fact, the more head downwards I am, the more I keep inventing new things."

"Now the cleverest thing of the sort that I ever did," he went on after a pause, "was inventing a new pudding during the meat-course."

"In time to have it cooked for the next course?" said Alice. "Well, not the next course," the Knight said in a slow thoughtful tone: "no, certainly not the next *course*."

"Then it would have to be the next day. I suppose you wouldn't have two pudding-courses in one dinner?"

"Well, not the *next* day," the Knight repeated as before: "not the next *day*. In fact," he went on, holding his head down, and his voice getting lower and lower, "I don't believe that pudding ever *was* cooked! In fact, I don't believe that pudding ever *will* be cooked! And yet it was a very clever pudding to invent."

"What did you mean it to be made of?" Alice asked, hoping to cheer him up, for the poor Knight seemed quite low-spirited about it.

"It began with blotting paper," the Knight answered with a groan.

"That wouldn't be very nice, I'm afraid –"

"Not very nice *alone*," he interrupted, quite eagerly: "but you've no idea what a difference it makes mixing it with other things – such as gunpowder and sealing-wax. And here I must leave you." They had just come to the end of the wood.

Alice could only look puzzled: she was thinking of the pudding.

"You are sad," the Knight said in an anxious tone: "let me sing you a song to comfort you."

"Is it very long?" Alice asked, for she had heard a good deal of poetry that day.

"It's long," said the Knight, "but very, *very* beautiful. Everybody that hears me sing it – either it brings the *tears* into their eyes, or else –"

"Or else what?" said Alice, for the Knight had made a sudden pause.

"Or else it doesn't, you know. The name of the song is called '*Haddocks' Eyes*.' "

"Oh, that's the name of the song, is it?" Alice said, trying to feel interested.

"No, you don't understand," the Knight said, looking a little vexed. "That's what the name is *called*. The name really is 'The Aged Aged Man.'"

"Then I ought to have said 'That's what the *song* is called'?" Alice corrected herself.

"No, you oughtn't: that's quite another thing! The *song* is called '*Ways And Means*': but that's only what it's *called*, you know!"

"Well, what *is* the song, then?" said Alice, who was by this time completely bewildered.

"I was coming to that," the Knight said. "The song really *is* '*A-Sitting On A Gate*': and the tune's my own invention."

 Key thoughts

- The White Knight's inventions are excellent, he just hasn't finished the building stage
- Make sure your problem really is what you think it is – don't try to solve a label
- Do steal ideas, but give credit where appropriate. Alice later noted that the tune wasn't his own invention.

index